FOUNDATIONS

Second Edition

LITERACY 8

 D0609658

Steven J. Molinsky • Bill Bliss

PEARSON
Longman

Foundations Literacy & Numeracy Workbook

Copyright © 2013 by Pearson Education, Inc.
All rights reserved.

No part of this publication may be reproduced, stored in a retrieval system, or transmitted in any form or by any means, electronic, mechanical, photocopying, recording, or otherwise, without the prior permission of the publisher.

Pearson Education, 10 Bank Street, White Plains, NY 10606

Editorial director: Pam Fishman
Director of special projects and digital initiatives: Aliza Greenblatt
Director of prepress: Liza Pleva
Senior manufacturing manager: Nancy Flaggman
Marketing director: Oliva Fernandez
Managing editor: Loretta Steeves
Production editor: Christine Cervoni, Camelot Editorial Services
Text design and composition: Wendy Wolf, Witz End Design
Cover design: Tracey Munz Cataldo, Wanda España, Warren Fischbach, Wendy Wolf
Illustrations: Richard E. Hill

ISBN-10: 0-13-294051-5
ISBN:13: 978-0-13-294051-1

Cover photo credits: (top left) Barry Rosenthal/Getty Images, (top middle left) Adam Gault/Photodisc/Getty Images, (bottom middle left) Image Source/Getty Images, (bottom left) Ciaran Griffin/Stockbyte/Getty Images, (right) Images.com/Corbis.

Printed in the United States of America

HOW TO ACCESS MP3 FILES ON THE CD-ROM

Windows Users:
1. Insert the CD-ROM into the CD-ROM drive of your computer.
2. Open "My Computer."
3. Right-click on the CD-ROM icon.
4. Click on Open.
5. Double-click on the mp3 file you would like to open.

Macintosh Users:
1. Insert the CD-ROM into the CD-ROM drive of your computer.
2. Click on the Foundations 2e WB icon that appears.
3. Double-click on the mp3 file you would like to open.

HOW TO ACCESS AUDIO TRACKS ON THE CD-ROM

Insert the CD-ROM into a CD player. It will play the CD Audio files.

Contents

1	Personal Information & Family	1
2	The Classroom	18
3	Everyday Activities & Weather	29
4	Numbers, Time, Calendar, Money	43
5	Home	60
6	Community	69
7	Describing	77
8	Food	85
9	Clothing, Colors, & Shopping	93
10	The Bank & the Post Office	101
11	Health	109
12	School	119
13	Work	127
14	Transportation	135
15	Recreation & Entertainment	143

Alphabet Practice: Upper Case Letters	151
Alphabet Practice: Lower Case Letters	156
Number Practice: Numbers 1–10	160
Listening Scripts	162
Answer Key	165
Correlation Key	172

A. Listen and say the alphabet. Track 2

A B C D E F G H I J K L M
N O P Q R S T U V W X Y Z

B. Listen and circle the letter you hear. Track 3

1. A   H   (J)   5. V   D   T
2. Z   E   P   6. Y   I   Z
3. C   G   B   7. M   N   V
4. Q   K   J   8. B   P   D

C. Listen and circle the correct name. Track 4

1. BLACK   (BLOCK)
2. WONG   FONG
3. LOUIS   LEWIS
4. ASMAR   ASMAL
5. VOSS   FOSS
6. CHEN   SHEN

Aa Bb Cc Dd Ee Ff Gg Hh Ii
Jj Kk Ll Mm Nn Oo Pp Qq Rr
Ss Tt Uu Vv Ww Xx Yy Zz

Circle the correct letter.

1. F   h   k   (f)   d

2. G   c   j   a   g

3. B   d   b   h   q

4. M   m   h   n   u

5. A   v   a   u   x

6. u   W   V   N   U

Circle the correct word.

1. LIST

   lest (list) lost last

2. NAME

   nice game mane name

3. YOUR

   year four your hour

4. SPELL

   spell spill spoil spool

5. PATEL

   Paver Pavel Patel Pater

6. SILVA

   Selva Silva Silve Silpa

Trace and copy.

L   L L L L

T   T T T T

I   I I I

H   H H H H

F   F F F

E   E E E

V   V V V

W   W W W W

A   A A A A

X   X X X

Y   Y Y Y

M   M M M M

N   N N N N

Z   Z Z Z

K   K K K

O   O O O

Q   Q Q Q

C   C C C

G   G G G

S   S S S

U   U U U

J   J J J J

D   D D D

P   P P P

B   B B B

R   R R R

* For practice with larger letters first, go to pages 151–155.

Trace and copy.

A A A A   N N N N

B B B B   O O O O

C C C C   P P P P

D D D D   Q Q Q Q

E E E E   R R R R

F F F F   S S S S

G G G G   T T T T

H H H H   U U U U

I I I I   V V V V

J J J J   W W W W

K K K K   X X X X

L L L L   Y Y Y Y

M M M M   Z Z Z Z

* For practice with larger letters first, go to pages 151–155.

Trace and copy.

l   l   l   l

u   u   u   u

b   b   b   b

v   v   v   v

d   d   d   d

w   w   w   w

h   h   h   h

x   x   x   x

k   k   k   k

z   z   z   z

f   f   f   f

i   i   i   i

t   t   t   t

r   r   r   r

o   o   o   o

s   s   s   s

c   c   c   c

p   p   p   p

e   e   e   e

q   q   q   q

a   a   a   a

g   g   g   g

n   n   n   n

j   j   j   j

m   m   m   m

y   y   y   y

* For practice with larger letters first, go to pages 156–159.

Trace and copy.

a a a a   n n n n

b b b b   o o o o

c c c c   p p p p

d d d d   q q q q

e e e e   r r r r

f f f f   s s s s

g g g g   t t t t

h h h h   u u u u

i i i i   v v v v

j j j j   w w w w

k k k k   x x x x

l l l l   y y y y

m m m m   z z z z

* For practice with larger letters first, go to pages 156–159.

A. Listen and say the numbers. Track 5

0   1   2   3   4

5   6   7   8   9

B. Listen and circle the number you hear. Track 6

1. (4)   9   5.   2   3
2.   6   7   6.   1   0
3.   5   9   7.   9   5
4.   9   6   8.   3   2

C. Listen and circle the correct answer. Track 7

1. 645-2219   (649-2215)
2. 424-1160   424-1168
3. 825-1212   825-2121
4. 917-0029   917-0025
5. 276-1284   276-1234
6. 796-3221   796-3231

Count the dots. Match.

10	three
1	four
6	seven
4	ten
7	five
8	one
9	two
3	eight
5	six
2	nine

Read, trace, and copy.

0 0 0 0

1 1 1 1

2 2 2 2

3 3 3 3

4 4 4 4

5 5 5 5

6 6 6 6

7 7 7 7

8 8 8 8

9 9 9 9

10 10 10 10

* For practice with larger numerals first, go to pages 160–161.

Read, trace, and copy.

zero   zero

one   one

two   two

three   three

four   four

five   five

six   six

seven   seven

eight   eight

nine   nine

ten   ten

Match.

1. name   90036

2. address   California

3. city   4G

4. state   8 Main St.

5. zip code   223-94-9148

6. apartment number   Los Angeles

7. telephone number   Marta Sanchez

8. social security number   (323) 723-4891

Choose the answer.

6 Center Street

1.
(A) city
(B) address
(C) name
(D) zip code

(646) 782-3394

2.
(A) state
(B) city
(C) zip code
(D) telephone number

Los Angeles

3.
(A) name
(B) state
(C) city
(D) address

90036

4.
(A) apartment number
(B) telephone number
(C) social security number
(D) zip code

David Lee

5.
(A) name
(B) city
(C) address
(D) state

025-93-2481

6.
(A) zip code
(B) social security number
(C) telephone number
(D) apartment number

Read, trace, and copy.

1. city · city ·

2. name · name ·

3. last · last ·

4. first · first ·

5. state · state ·

6. street · street ·

7. number · number ·

8. address · address ·

9. telephone · telephone ·

10. apartment · apartment ·

Circle the words. Then write the sentences.

(My)(name)(is)(Rosa).

My name is Rosa.

1. MyfirstnameisJenny.

2. MylastnameisChen.

3. Myaddressis6MainStreet.

4. Myapartmentnumberis7.

5. Nicetomeetyou.

A. Look at page 3 of *Foundations*. Write the missing word.

1. My _____ is Anna Ramos.

2. My _____ name is Anna.

3. My _____ name is Ramos.

4. My _____ is 4 Main Street.

5. My _____ number is 2F.

6. My telephone _____ is (323) 456-8917.

7. My _____ security number is 226-37-4189.

8. My _____ code is 90036.

B. Look at page 12 of *Foundations*. Circle the correct word.

1. He's my (father   mother).

2. She's my (son   daughter).

3. She's my (mother   father).

4. She's my (grandmother   grandfather).

5. He's my (brother   sister).

6. She's my (husband   wife).

7. He's my (sister   husband).

8. He's my (grandmother   grandfather).

9. She's my (granddaughter   grandson).

A. Fill out the form. Use capital (upper case) letters.

NAME: _____
FIRST   LAST

ADDRESS: _____
NUMBER   STREET   APT.

_____
CITY   STATE   ZIP CODE

TELEPHONE NUMBER: _____

SOCIAL SECURITY NUMBER: _____

B. Fill out the form. Use upper case and lower case letters.

NAME
FIRST   LAST

ADDRESS
NUMBER   STREET   APT.

CITY   STATE   ZIP CODE

TELEPHONE NUMBER

SOCIAL SECURITY NUMBER

Listen and choose the correct picture. Track 8

1.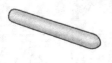
   (A)   (B)   (C)

2.
   (A)   (B)   (C)

3.
   (A)   (B)   (C)

4.
   (A)   (B)   (C)

5.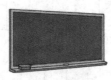
   (A)   (B)   (C)

6.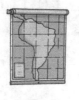
   (A)   (B)   (C)

ANSWERS
1 Ⓐ Ⓑ **Ⓒ**
2 Ⓐ Ⓑ Ⓒ
3 Ⓐ Ⓑ Ⓒ
4 Ⓐ Ⓑ Ⓒ
5 Ⓐ Ⓑ Ⓒ
6 Ⓐ Ⓑ Ⓒ

Match.

1.    pen

2.    clock

3.   computer

4.    globe

5.   map

6.   notebook

7.   pencil

8.   ruler

pen

1.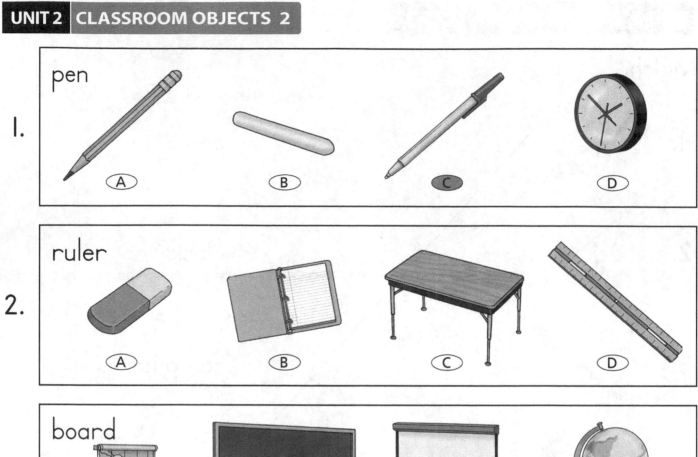

A   B   C   D

ruler

2.

A   B   C   D

board

3.

A   B   C   D

desk

4.

A   B   C   D

calculator

5.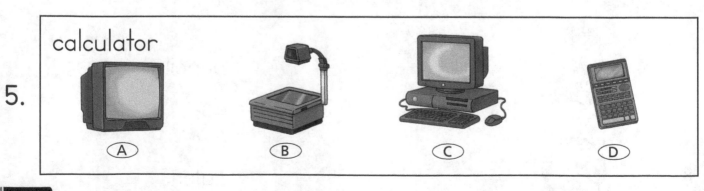

A   B   C   D

Read, trace, and copy.

1. pen   pen

2. map   map

3. desk   desk

4. wall   wall

5. book   book

6. chair   chair

7. clock   clock

8. globe   globe

9. board   board

10. eraser   eraser

Match.

1.

Write your name.

2.

Stand up.

3.

Sit down.

4.

Go to the board.

5.

Raise your hand.

6.

Put away your book.

7.

Open your book.

8.

Erase your name.

A. Listen and choose the correct picture. **Track 9** 🔊

1.

   Ⓐ   Ⓑ   Ⓒ

2.

   Ⓐ   Ⓑ   Ⓒ

3.

   Ⓐ   Ⓑ   Ⓒ

4.

   Ⓐ   Ⓑ   Ⓒ

ANSWERS		
1 Ⓐ	Ⓑ	Ⓒ
2 Ⓐ	Ⓑ	Ⓒ
3 Ⓐ	Ⓑ	Ⓒ
4 Ⓐ	Ⓑ	Ⓒ

B. Listen and say the numbers. **Track 10** 🔊

11	12	13	14	15	16	17	18	19

C. Listen and circle the number you hear. **Track 11** 🔊

1. ⑬   18   5.   11   17

2. 11   12   6.   15   16

3. 16   19   7.   7   17

4. 14   15   8.   8   18

Match.

1. sixteen   19

2. nineteen   14

3. eleven   13

4. seventeen   16

5. fourteen   15

6. eighteen   11

7. twelve   17

8. thirteen   12

9. fifteen   18

Read, trace, and copy.

11 11 11 11

12 12 12 12

13 13 13 13

14 14 14 14

15 15 15 15

16 16 16 16

17 17 17 17

18 18 18 18

19 19 19 19

Read, trace, and copy.

1. eleven   eleven

2. twelve   twelve

3. thirteen   thirteen

4. fourteen   fourteen

5. fifteen   fifteen

6. sixteen   sixteen

7. seventeen   seventeen

8. eighteen   eighteen

9. nineteen   nineteen

Circle the words. Then write the sentences.

Close your book.

<u>Close your book.</u>

1. Raiseyourhand.

2. Writeyourname.

3. Theclockisonthewall.

4. Isthisyournotebook?

5. Therearebooksonmydesk.

A. Look at pages 18–19 of *Foundations*. Write the missing letters. Then say the words.

1. m__p
2. p__n
3. d__sk
4. cl__ck
5. p__ncil
6. w__ll

7. n__tebook
8. gl__be
9. t__ble
10. r__ler
11. st__dent
12. scr____n

B. Look at page 26 of *Foundations*. Write the missing words. Then say the sentences.

1. Raise your _____.
2. Open your _____.
3. Write your _____.
4. Go to the _____.
5. Sit _____.
6. Stand _____.
7. _____ out your book.
8. _____ away your book.

A. Listen and write the number under the correct picture. Track 12

_____   _____   _____

_____   _____   _____

B. Listen and write the number under the correct picture. Track 13

_____   _____   _____

_____   _____   _____

Match.

1.   I go to school.

2.    I iron.

3.    I brush my teeth.

4.    I exercise.

5.    I get dressed.

6.    I play basketball.

7.    I eat lunch.

8.    I get up.

1. comb my hair

2. read

3. watch TV

4. do the laundry

5. play the guitar

1. Ⓐ comb my hair
    Ⓑ brush my teeth
    Ⓒ take a shower
    Ⓓ wash the dishes

2. Ⓐ get dressed
    Ⓑ get up
    Ⓒ exercise
    Ⓓ go to bed

3. Ⓐ study
    Ⓑ come home
    Ⓒ do the laundry
    Ⓓ go to school

4. Ⓐ eat breakfast
    Ⓑ read
    Ⓒ eat dinner
    Ⓓ make lunch

5. Ⓐ listen to music
    Ⓑ play the guitar
    Ⓒ play basketball
    Ⓓ watch TV

6. Ⓐ feed the baby
    Ⓑ walk the dog
    Ⓒ take a shower
    Ⓓ go to work

Read, trace, and copy.

1. eat   eat

2. read   read

3. cook   cook

4. wash   wash

5. iron   iron

6. play   play

7. study   study

8. clean   clean

9. lunch   lunch

10. dinner   dinner

Match.

1.

2.

3.

4.

5.

6.

7.

It's cold.

It's snowing.

It's sunny.

It's hot.

It's raining.

It's foggy.

It's cloudy.

Read, trace, and copy.

1. hot   hot

2. cold   cold

3. sunny   sunny

4. foggy   foggy

5. cloudy   cloudy

6. raining   raining

7. snowing   snowing

8. weather   weather

A. Listen and say the numbers. **Track 14**

20	21	22	23	24	25	26	27	28	29
30	40	50	60	70	80	90	100		

B. Listen and circle the number you hear. **Track 15**

1. 22   23
2. 50   60
3. 25   29

4. 30   40
5. 28   80
6. 40   24

C. Listen and say each group of numbers. **Track 16**

2	12	20
3	13	30
4	14	40
5	15	50

6	16	60
7	17	70
8	18	80
9	19	90

D. Listen and circle the number you hear. **Track 17**

1. 5   15   50
2. 8   18   80
3. 3   13   30

4. 24   34   44
5. 17   70   71
6. 55   50   59

Circle the correct number.

1. | three | ③ | 13 | 30 |

2. | sixty | 6 | 16 | 60 |

3. | seventeen | 7 | 17 | 70 |

4. | eight | 8 | 18 | 80 |

5. | nineteen | 9 | 19 | 90 |

6. | fifty | 5 | 15 | 50 |

7. | fourteen | 4 | 14 | 40 |

8. | twelve | 2 | 12 | 20 |

9. | thirty | 3 | 13 | 30 |

10. | fifty-three | 33 | 53 | 55 |

Read, trace, and copy.

20 20 20 20 -------------------------------------

21 21 21 21 -------------------------------------

22 22 22 22 -------------------------------------

23 23 23 23 -------------------------------------

24 24 24 24 -------------------------------------

25 25 25 25 -------------------------------------

26 26 26 26 -------------------------------------

27 27 27 27 -------------------------------------

28 28 28 28 -------------------------------------

29 29 29 29 -------------------------------------

Read, trace, and copy. Then say the numbers to count by 10.

10 10 10 10

20 20 20 20

30 30 30 30

40 40 40 40

50 50 50 50

60 60 60 60

70 70 70 70

80 80 80 80

90 90 90 90

100 100 100

Write the correct number.

1. 1   2   3   4   5

2. 6   7   ___   9   10

3. 11   ___   13   14   15

4. 16   17   18   ___   20

5. 10   20   30   40   ___

6. 60   70   ___   90   100

7. 22   ___   24   25   26

8. 55   56   57   ___   59

9. 14   ___   16   17   18

Circle the words. Then write the sentences.

I eat dinner.

1. Ibrushmyteeth.

2. Igotoschool.

3. EverydayImakelunch.

4. Whatareyoudoing?

5. Myfatherwashesthedishes.

A. Look at page 32 of *Foundations*. Write the missing word.

1. Every day I _____ a shower.
2. Every day I _____ my teeth.
3. I comb my _____ every day.
4. Every day I get up and eat _____.
5. I _____ to work every day.
6. I _____ TV every day.
7. I get undressed and go to _____.
8. I _____ dinner for my family every day.

B. Look at page 33 of *Foundations*. Write the missing word.

1. I _____ the dishes.
2. I _____ basketball.
3. I _____ the laundry.
4. I feed the _____.
5. I walk the _____.
6. I listen to _____.
7. I play the _____.
8. I _____ breakfast for my son and daughter.

A. Listen and circle the number you hear. Track 18

1. 455   1455
2. 723   1723
3. 1381   3081
4. 1216   1260

5. 114   140
6. 313   330
7. 215   250
8. 204   240

B. Listen and choose the correct clock. Track 19

1.

   A   B   C

2.

   A   B   C

3.

   A   B   C

4.

   A   B   C

ANSWERS		
1 Ⓐ	Ⓑ	Ⓒ
2 Ⓐ	Ⓑ	Ⓒ
3 Ⓐ	Ⓑ	Ⓒ
4 Ⓐ	Ⓑ	Ⓒ

Match.

 1.

3:30

 2.

1:45

 3.

7:15

 4.

10:00

 5.

11:30

 6.

2:00

 7.

8:45

 8.

4:15

8:30

1.

A   B   C   D

10:00

2.

A   B   C   D

2:45

3.

A   B   C   D

6:15

4.

A   B   C   D

12:30

5.

A   B   C   D

A. Match.

1. SUN   Thursday

2. TUE   Wednesday

3. THU   Sunday

4. SAT   Saturday

5. WED   Friday

6. FRI   Tuesday

7. MON   Monday

B. Put the days of the week in the correct order.

___ Saturday   ___ Tuesday

___ Friday   ___ Wednesday

___ Monday   _1_ Sunday

___ Thursday

A. Read, trace, and copy.

Sunday   Sunday

Monday   Monday

Tuesday   Tuesday

Wednesday   Wednesday

Thursday   Thursday

Friday   Friday

Saturday   Saturday

7:00   7:00   4:30   4:30

6:15   6:15   9:45   9:45

B. Write the time.

_____   _____   _____   _____

47

A. Listen and say the ordinal numbers. Track 20

1st	2nd	3rd	4th	5th	6th	7th	8th	9th	10th
11th	12th	13th	14th	15th	16th	17th	18th	19th	20th
21st	22nd	30th	40th	50th	60th	70th	80th	90th	100th

B. Listen and circle the number you hear. Track 21

1. 16th   60th
2. 2nd   7th
3. 3rd   30th

4. 4th   40th
5. 31st   33rd
6. 52nd   57th

C. Listen and say each pair of numbers. Track 22

1 1st	5 5th	8 8th
2 2nd	6 6th	9 9th
3 3rd	7 7th	10 10th
4 4th		

D. Listen and circle the number you hear. Track 23

1. 21   21st
2. 50   50th
3. 18   18th

4. 9   9th
5. 10   10th
6. 6   6th

A. Match.

1. fourth   80th

2. seventh   50th

3. fiftieth   12th

4. eightieth   7th

5. fifth   4th

6. twelfth   5th

B. Read, trace, and copy.

1st 1st	6th 6th
2nd 2nd	7th 7th
3rd 3rd	8th 8th
4th 4th	9th 9th
5th 5th	10th 10th

Match.

1. MAY		March
2. SEP		January
3. MAR		June
4. JUL		November
5. APR		August
6. AUG		December
7. OCT		February
8. NOV		April
9. JAN		May
10. JUN		September
11. DEC		October
12. FEB		July

MAR

1. March — (A)   May — (B)   Monday — (C)   November — (D)

SEP

2. Saturday — (A)   Sunday — (B)   December — (C)   September — (D)

JUL

3. January — (A)   June — (B)   Tuesday — (C)   July — (D)

THU

4. Fourth — (A)   Tuesday — (B)   Thursday — (C)   Friday — (D)

OCT

5. October — (A)   August — (B)   April — (C)   November — (D)

SAT

6. June — (A)   Sunny — (B)   Saturday — (C)   Sunday — (D)

Read, trace, and copy.

January January

February February

March March

April April

May May

June June

July July

August August

September September

October October

November November

December December

A. Match.

1.    May 22, 2015

2.    July 7, 2015

3.    February 3, 2015

4.    March 22, 2015

5.    January 7, 2015

6.    June 7, 2015

B. Write the dates.

1.  _____   3.  _____

2. _____   4. _____

A. Match.

1. July 12, 2016   10/4/15

2. October 4, 2015   12/7/14

3. June 8, 2015   8/6/15

4. December 7, 2014   6/8/15

5. April 10, 2015   7/12/16

6. August 6, 2015   4/10/15

B. Write the dates.

1. 1/14/15 _____

2. 6/25/14 _____

3. 3/7/16 _____

4. 9/25/13 _____

C. Write the dates as numbers.

1. March 12, 2015 _____   5. November 16, 2014 _____

2. July 4, 2017 _____   6. January 11, 2013 _____

3. May 17, 2016 _____   7. September 9, 2015 _____

4. April 15, 2015 _____   8. August 20, 2016 _____

Match.

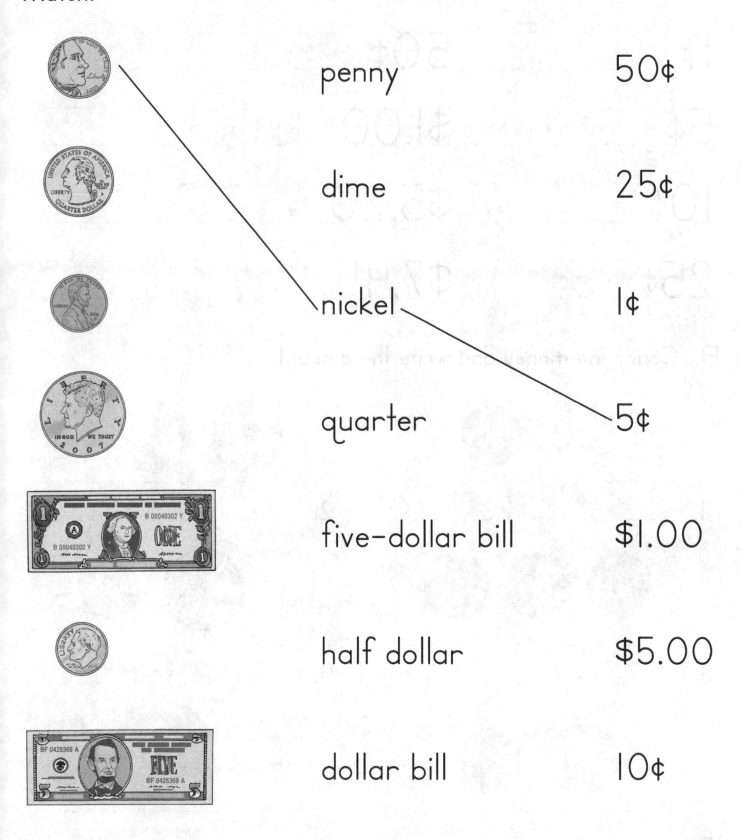

penny   50¢

dime   25¢

nickel   1¢

quarter   5¢

five-dollar bill $1.00

half dollar $5.00

dollar bill   10¢

A. Read, trace, and copy.

1¢   1¢

5¢   5¢

10¢   10¢

25¢   25¢

50¢   50¢

$1.00 $1.00

$5.20 $5.20

$7.45 $7.45

B. Count the money and write the amount.

1.

   20¢

2.

3.

4.

5.

6.

Count the money and write the amount.

1. $25.00

2. _____

3. _____

4. _____

5. _____

6. _____

7. _____

8. _____

9. _____

10. _____

Circle the words. Then write the sentences.

What month is it?

1. Whattimeisit?

2. IaminApartmentseven.

3. MybirthdayisJunefirst.

4. Whendoyougotoschool?

5. Whatfloordoyouliveon?

A. Look at page 52 of *Foundations*. Write the day.

1. FRI _____   5. MON _____
2. SUN _____   6. THU _____
3. TUE _____   7. WED _____
4. SAT _____

B. Look at page 56 of *Foundations*. Write the month.

1. MAR _____   7. MAY _____
2. JUN _____   8. FEB _____
3. AUG _____   9. APR _____
4. JAN _____   10. JUL _____
5. NOV _____   11. OCT _____
6. SEP _____   12. DEC _____

C. Write the correct month.

1. The third month of the year is _____.
2. The seventh month of the year is _____.
3. The fifth month of the year is _____.
4. The first month of the year is _____.
5. The tenth month of the year is _____.
6. The twelfth month of the year is _____.

Listen and choose the correct picture. **Track 24** 🔊

1.
    Ⓐ　　　　　　　　Ⓑ　　　　　　　　Ⓒ

2.
    Ⓐ　　　　　　　　Ⓑ　　　　　　　　Ⓒ

3.
    Ⓐ　　　　　　　　Ⓑ　　　　　　　　Ⓒ

4.
    Ⓐ　　　　　　　　Ⓑ　　　　　　　　Ⓒ

5.
    Ⓐ　　　　　　　　Ⓑ　　　　　　　　Ⓒ

6.
    Ⓐ　　　　　　　　Ⓑ　　　　　　　　Ⓒ

ANSWERS		
1 Ⓐ	Ⓑ	Ⓒ
2 Ⓐ	Ⓑ	Ⓒ
3 Ⓐ	Ⓑ	Ⓒ
4 Ⓐ	Ⓑ	Ⓒ
5 Ⓐ	Ⓑ	Ⓒ
6 Ⓐ	Ⓑ	Ⓒ

Match.

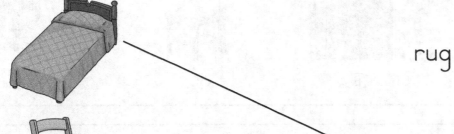

1.

2.   rug

                                              bed

3.

                                              lamp

4.

                                              sofa

5.

                                              refrigerator

6.

                                              table

7.   chair

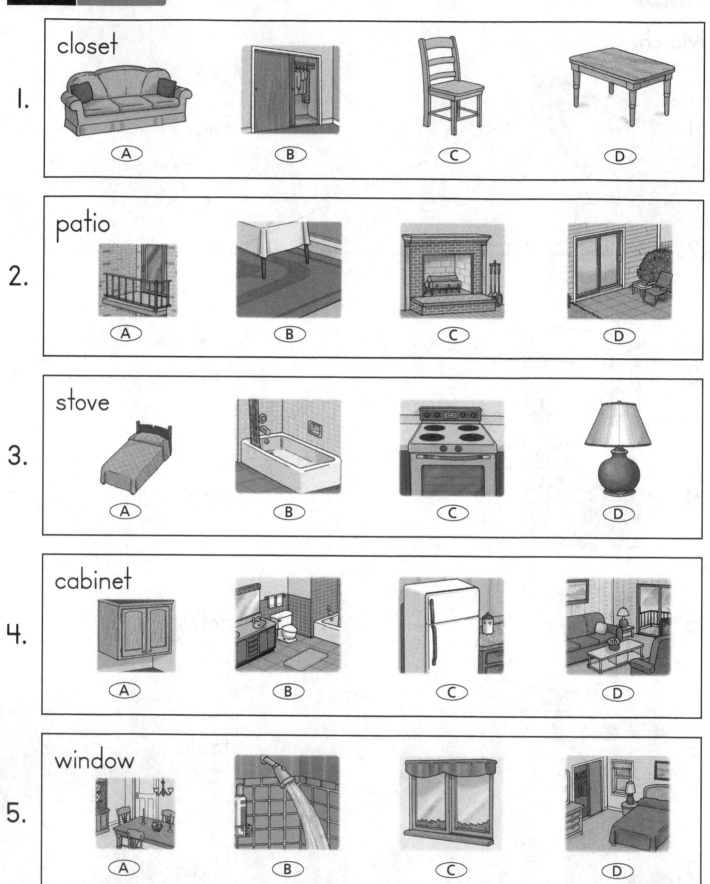

1. closet
   A B C D

2. patio
   A B C D

3. stove
   A B C D

4. cabinet
   A B C D

5. window
   A B C D

1. Ⓐ bedroom
    Ⓑ bathroom
    Ⓒ dining room
    Ⓓ kitchen

2. Ⓐ bedroom
    Ⓑ dining room
    Ⓒ balcony
    Ⓓ patio

3. Ⓐ closet
    Ⓑ building
    Ⓒ bathroom
    Ⓓ kitchen

4. Ⓐ patio
    Ⓑ dining room
    Ⓒ kitchen
    Ⓓ living room

5. Ⓐ living room
    Ⓑ shower
    Ⓒ duplex
    Ⓓ fireplace

6. Ⓐ dormitory
    Ⓑ balcony
    Ⓒ table
    Ⓓ patio

Read, trace, and copy.

1. rug   rug

2. bed   bed

3. lamp   lamp

4. chair   chair

5. table   table

6. stove   stove

7. closet   closet

8. shower   shower

9. bedroom   bedroom

10. bathroom   bathroom

Write the word.

1. _____

2. _____

3. _____

4. _____

5. _____

6. _____

7. _____

8. _____

Circle the correct number.

1. I live in Apartment | 10   10th |.

2. My apartment is on the | 8   8th | floor.

3. There are | 2   2nd | windows in my bedroom.

4. I live on | 6   6th | Avenue.

5. This dining room table has | 4   4th | chairs.

6. This apartment has | 3   3rd | bedrooms.

7. I live on the | 1   1st | floor.

8. I live in Apartment | 9   9th |.

9. A duplex has | 2   2nd | homes.

Circle the words. Then write the sentences.

(Put)(it)(in)(the)(dining)(room).

Put it in the dining room.

1. Iliveinanapartmentbuilding.

2. IwatchTVinthelivingroom.

3. Myapartmenthasanicebathroom.

4. Thereisaclosetinthebedroom.

5. Wheredoyouwantthisrug?

A. Look at pages 64-65 of *Foundations*. Write the missing letters. Then say the words.

1. b_d
2. r_g
3. l_mp
4. w_ndow
5. cl_set

6. t_ble
7. s_fa
8. st_ve
9. f_replace
10. d_ning room

B. Look at page 75 of *Foundations*. Write the correct word.

1. There's a stove in the _____.
2. There's a bathtub in the _____.
3. A girl is studying in her _____.
4. There's a dog on the _____.
5. There's a TV in the _____.

C. Circle the correct word.

1. I live in a nice apartment (floor   building).
2. There's a (shower   sofa) in my bathroom.
3. There's a new (bathtub   stove) in our kitchen.
4. Please put the table in the (dining room   fireplace).
5. There's a nice (patio   closet) in the bedroom.

A. Listen and write the number under the correct picture. Track 25 🔊

_____

_____

_____

_____

_____

_____

B. Listen and write the number under the correct picture. Track 26 🔊

_____

_____

_____

_____

_____

_____

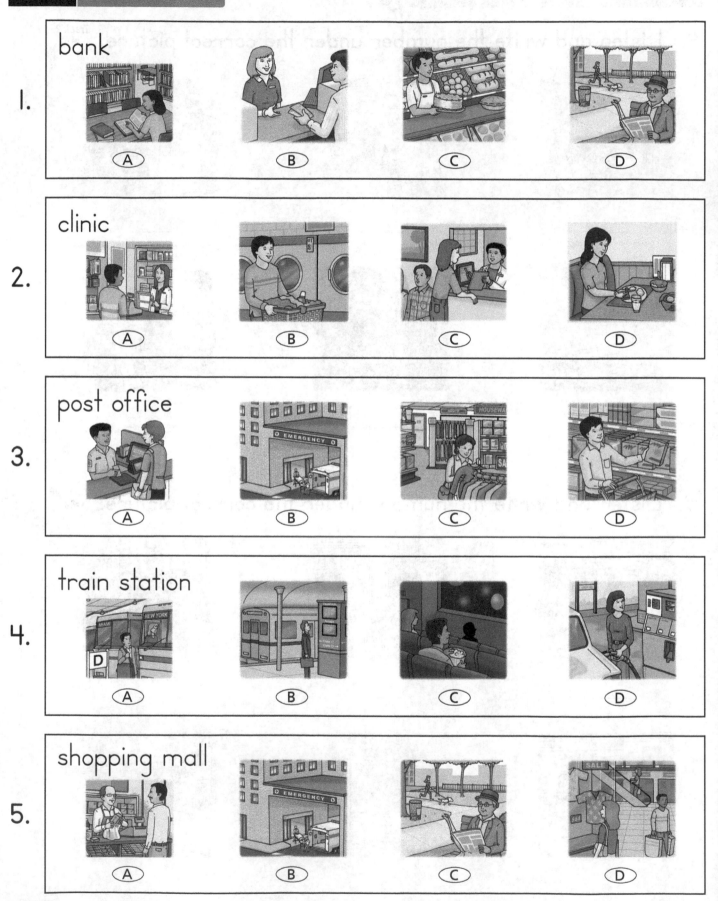

1. bank
   A B C D

2. clinic
   A B C D

3. post office
   A B C D

4. train station
   A B C D

5. shopping mall
   A B C D

1. (A) bank
   (B) post office
   (C) grocery store
   (D) library

2. (A) laundromat
   (B) shopping mall
   (C) hospital
   (D) park

3. (A) bakery
   (B) restaurant
   (C) drug store
   (D) clinic

4. (A) supermarket
   (B) restaurant
   (C) hospital
   (D) movie theater

5. (A) laundromat
   (B) gas station
   (C) train station
   (D) bus station

6. (A) drug store
   (B) hospital
   (C) bakery
   (D) bank

Read, trace, and copy.

1. park   park

2. bank   bank

3. clinic   clinic

4. store   store

5. bakery   bakery

6. library   library

7. school   school

8. station   station

9. hospital   hospital

10. restaurant   restaurant

Write the word.

1. _____

2. _____

3. _____

4. _____

5. _____

6. _____

7. _____

8. _____

1. How many apartments are there in the building?
   (A) 6   (C) 8
   (B) 7   (D) 9

2. How many floors are there in the building?
   (A) 2   (C) 8
   (B) 4   (D) 16

3. How many closets are there in the bedroom?
   (A) 1   (C) 3
   (B) 2   (D) 4

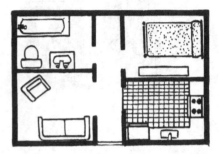

4. How many rooms are there in the apartment?
   (A) 1   (C) 5
   (B) 4   (D) 6

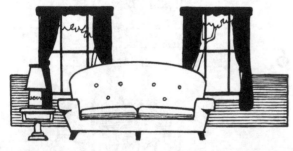

5. How many windows are there in the living room?
   (A) 2   (C) 6
   (B) 4   (D) 12

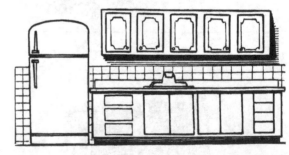

6. How many cabinets are there in the kitchen?
   (A) 1   (C) 4
   (B) 2   (D) 5

Circle the words. Then write the sentences.

The library is on Main Street.

1. I am going to the post office.

2. They are eating at a restaurant.

3. The bus station is next to the park.

4. The clinic is across from the bank.

5. Is there a laundromat nearby?

A. Look at pages 76–77 of *Foundations*. Write the missing word.

1. bus _____

2. post _____

3. shopping _____

4. grocery _____

5. gas _____

6. movie _____

7. department _____

8. train _____

9. drug _____

B. Look at page 87 of *Foundations*. Write the correct word.

1. A man is buying stamps at the _____.

2. A woman is reading a book in the _____.

3. A man is buying medicine in the _____.

4. A woman is washing her clothes at the _____.

5. A woman is in her car at the _____.

6. A man and a woman are eating at a _____.

7. A woman and a man are buying food at the _____.

8. Children are playing basketball in the _____.

9. A man is putting money in the _____.

A. Listen and choose the correct picture. Track 27

1.
   Ⓐ   Ⓑ   Ⓒ

2.
   Ⓐ   Ⓑ   Ⓒ

3.
   Ⓐ   Ⓑ   Ⓒ

4.
   Ⓐ   Ⓑ   Ⓒ

ANSWERS		
1 Ⓐ	Ⓑ	Ⓒ
2 Ⓐ	Ⓑ	Ⓒ
3 Ⓐ	Ⓑ	Ⓒ
4 Ⓐ	Ⓑ	Ⓒ

B. Listen and write the number under the correct picture. Track 28

_____ _____ _____ _____

Match.

1.    tired

2.   hungry

3.    angry

4.   afraid

5.   happy

6.    thirsty

7.   sick

8.   sad

1.
   (A) angry
   (B) afraid
   (C) sick
   (D) happy

2.
   (A) hungry
   (B) thirsty
   (C) sad
   (D) tired

3.
   (A) tired
   (B) thirsty
   (C) angry
   (D) hungry

4.
   (A) tired
   (B) afraid
   (C) sick
   (D) sad

5.
   (A) thirsty
   (B) tired
   (C) sick
   (D) sad

6.
   (A) hungry
   (B) afraid
   (C) happy
   (D) angry

Read, trace, and copy.

1. old   old

2. tall   tall

3. hair   hair

4. eyes   eyes

5. short   short

6. young   young

7. single   single

8. height   height

9. hungry   hungry

10. married   married

A. Write the word.

1. _____

2. _____

3. _____

4. _____

B. Fill out the form.

(Please print)

NAME _____ ____ _____
First   MI   Last

ADDRESS _____
Number   Street

_____ _____ _____
City   State   Zip Code

COUNTRY OF ORIGIN _____   **LANGUAGE(S)** _____

(Circle)

HAIR COLOR: Black   Brown   Blond   Red   White   Gray

EYE COLOR: Brown   Blue   Black   Green   Other: _____

MARITAL STATUS: Single   Married   Divorced   Widowed

SIGNATURE _____   **TODAY'S DATE** |__|__|__|__|__|
                                                                Month Day Year

1. What's your weight?

   35 years old.   150 pounds.   5 feet 9 inches.

   Ⓐ   Ⓑ   Ⓒ

2. What's your height?

   160 pounds.   22 years old.   4 feet 11 inches.

   Ⓐ   Ⓑ   Ⓒ

3. What's your age?

   5 feet 10 inches.   41 years old.   133 pounds.

   Ⓐ   Ⓑ   Ⓒ

4. How old are you?

   126 pounds.   6 feet.   19 years old.

   Ⓐ   Ⓑ   Ⓒ

5. How tall are you?

   5 feet 10 inches.   137 pounds.   32 years old.

   Ⓐ   Ⓑ   Ⓒ

6. How much do you weigh?

   5 feet 9 inches.   125 pounds.   18 years old.

   Ⓐ   Ⓑ   Ⓒ

Circle the words. Then write the sentences.

My daughter is short.

1. Ourchildrenaretall.

_____

2. Mybrotherismarried.

_____

3. Shehasbrowneyesandblackhair.

_____

4. Whatdoesshelooklike?

_____

5. Whatlanguagedoyouspeak?

_____

A. Match the opposites.

1. young   married
2. short   happy
3. thin   old
4. sad   heavy
5. single   tall

B. Circle the correct word.

1. He has (angry   curly) hair.
2. My daughter has blond (hair   eyes).
3. She isn't tall or short. She's average (weight   height).
4. I go to the clinic when I'm (sick   tired).
5. He speaks (Mexico   Spanish).
6. She speaks (Brazil   Portuguese).
7. I'm from (China   Chinese).
8. Where are you (speak   from)?
9. What (language   country) do you speak?
10. I'm not young or old. I'm (average height   middle-aged).
11. My son has curly red (eyes   hair).
12. He's not thin or heavy. He's average (weight   height).

A. Listen and write the number under the correct picture. 🔊 Track 29

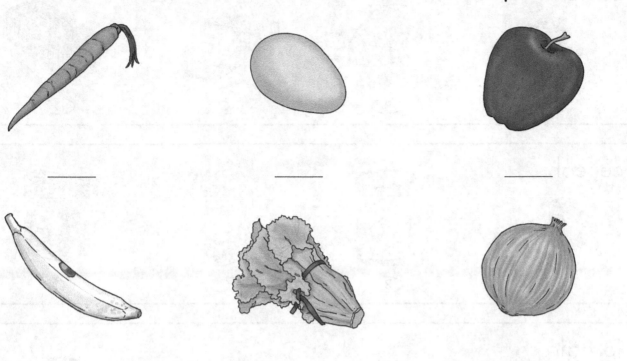

_____ _____ _____

_____ _____ _____

B. Listen and write the number under the correct picture. 🔊 Track 30

_____ _____ _____

_____ _____ _____

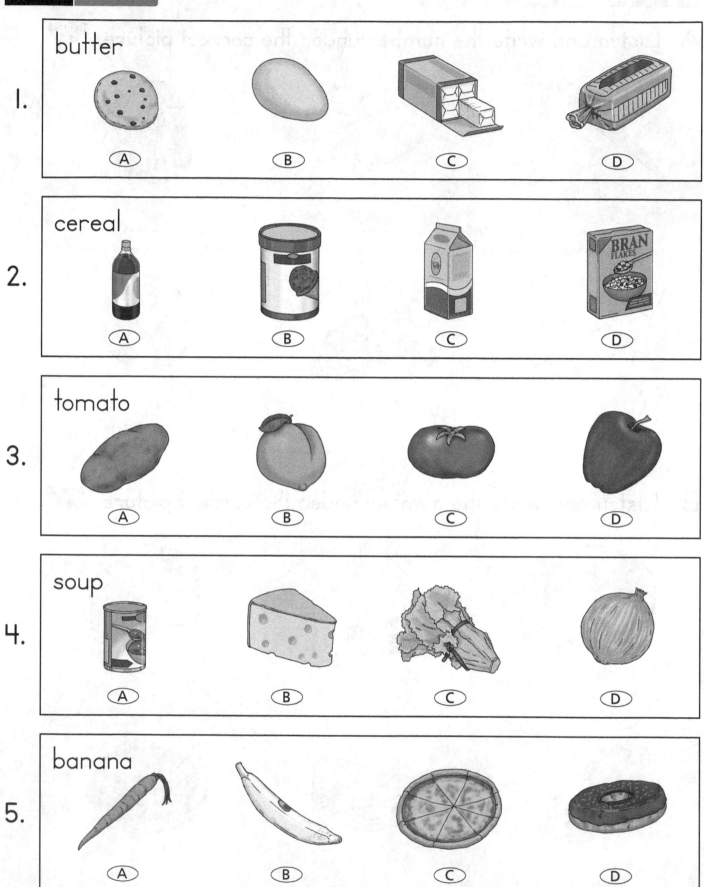

butter
1. A B C D

cereal
2. A B C D

tomato
3. A B C D

soup
4. A B C D

banana
5. A B C D

1. Ⓐ hot dog
   Ⓑ taco
   Ⓒ hamburger
   Ⓓ cereal

2. Ⓐ peach
   Ⓑ pizza
   Ⓒ potato
   Ⓓ taco

3. Ⓐ hamburger
   Ⓑ cheeseburger
   Ⓒ cheese
   Ⓓ sandwich

4. Ⓐ lemonade
   Ⓑ milk
   Ⓒ lettuce
   Ⓓ cereal

5. Ⓐ soda
   Ⓑ coffee
   Ⓒ milk
   Ⓓ ice cream

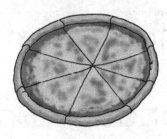

6. Ⓐ pizza
   Ⓑ sandwich
   Ⓒ taco
   Ⓓ hot dog

Read, trace, and copy.

1. milk   milk

2. taco   taco

3. soup   soup

4. onion   onion

5. bread   bread

6. apple   apple

7. orange   orange

8. potato   potato

9. lemonade   lemonade

10. sandwich   sandwich

Write the word.

1. _____

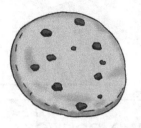

2. _____

3. _____

4. _____

5. _____

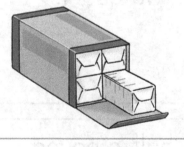

6. _____

7. _____

8. _____

1. one pound

   1 lb.   1 qt.   1 doz.

   (A)   (B)   (C)

2. two pounds

   2 qts.   1 lb.   2 lbs.

   (A)   (B)   (C)

3. a dozen eggs

   2 eggs   6 eggs   12 eggs

   (A)   (B)   (C)

4. two quarts

   2 doz.   2 qts.   2 lbs.

   (A)   (B)   (C)

5. half a pound

   1/2 lb.   1/2 qt.   1/2 doz.

   (A)   (B)   (C)

6. half a dozen

   1 doz.   1/2 doz.   1/2 lb.

   (A)   (B)   (C)

Circle the words. Then write the sentences.

Carrots are in Aisle One.

Carrots are in Aisle One.

1. Oranges are in Aisle Two.

2. Are there any onions?

3. What are you looking for?

4. We need a box of cereal.

5. Please get a pound of tomatoes.

A. Write these words in the correct categories.

apple	butter	donut	onion
banana	cheese	lettuce	orange
bread	cookie	milk	potato

Fruits   Vegetables

_____   _____

_____   _____

_____   _____

Baked Goods   Dairy

_____   _____

_____   _____

_____   _____

B. Circle the correct word.

1. We need a bunch of (milk   bananas).

2. We need a (loaf   quart) of bread.

3. Please get a dozen (cereal   eggs).

4. Please get a (bag   jar) of sugar.

5. I'm thirsty. I'd like (mayonnaise   lemonade), please.

A. Listen and write the number under the correct picture. Track 31 🔊

———

———

———

———

———

———

B. Listen and write the number under the correct picture. Track 32 🔊

———

———

———

———

———

———

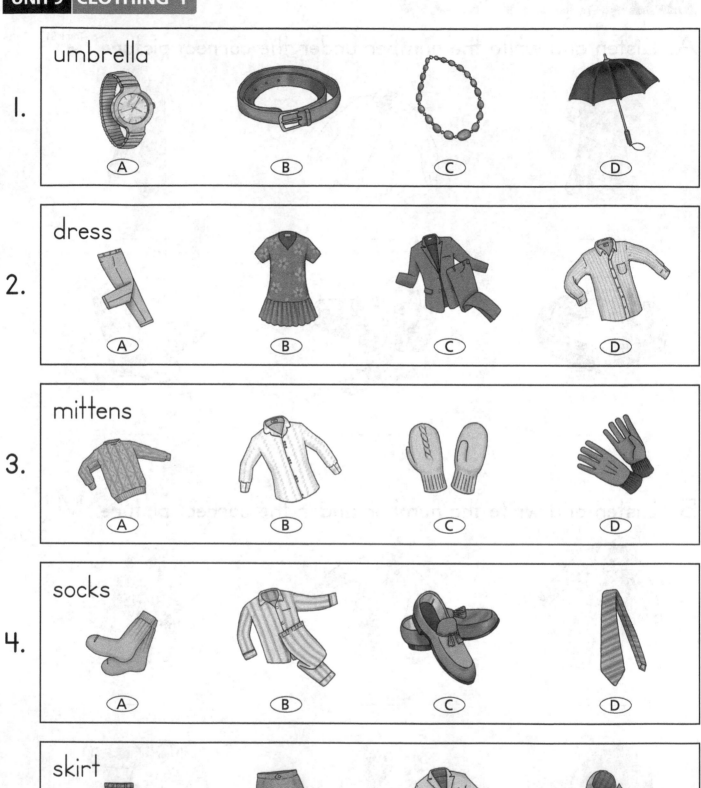

1. umbrella

A B C D

2. dress

A B C D

3. mittens

A B C D

4. socks

A B C D

5. skirt

A B C D

1. Ⓐ socks
   Ⓑ shirts
   Ⓒ suits
   Ⓓ shoes

2. Ⓐ shirt
   Ⓑ coat
   Ⓒ sweater
   Ⓓ jacket

3. Ⓐ blouse
   Ⓑ dress
   Ⓒ sweater
   Ⓓ coat

4. Ⓐ socks
   Ⓑ mittens
   Ⓒ gloves
   Ⓓ jeans

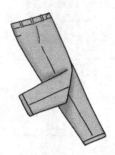

5. Ⓐ gloves
   Ⓑ pants
   Ⓒ pajamas
   Ⓓ suits

6. Ⓐ umbrella
   Ⓑ necklace
   Ⓒ watch
   Ⓓ belt

Read, trace, and copy.

1. coat   coat

2. dress   dress

3. shoes   shoes

4. socks   socks

5. blouse   blouse

6. gloves   gloves

7. umbrella   umbrella

8. necklace   necklace

9. sweater   sweater

10. pajamas   pajamas

Write the word.

1. _____

2. _____

3. _____

4. _____

5. _____

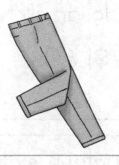

6. _____

7. _____

8. _____

1. fifty dollars and fifteen cents

   $50.50 $15.15 $15.50 $50.15

   A   B   C   D

2. thirteen dollars and fourteen cents

   $30.14 $13.14 $14.30 $14.13

   A   B   C   D

3. seven ninety-five

   $79.50 $70.95 $7.95 $70.59

   A   B   C   D

4. a dollar sixty

   $1.60 $60.00 $160.00 $60.60

   A   B   C   D

5. fourteen eighty-nine

   $140.89 $14.98 $40.89 $14.89

   A   B   C   D

6. five fifty-five

   $50.55 $50.05 $5.55 $5.50

   A   B   C   D

Circle the words. Then write the sentences.

(Umbrellas)(are)(over)(there).

Umbrellas are over there.

1. MayIhelpyou?

_____

2. Theshirtistoolarge.

_____

3. Myfavoritecolorisorange.

_____

4. Watchesareonthethirdfloor.

_____

5. Whatsizedressdoyouwear?

_____

A. Write these words in the correct categories.

blue	large	small
brown	medium	socks
dress	pajamas	yellow

Clothing   Colors

_____   _____

_____   _____

_____   _____

Sizes

_____

_____

_____

B. Circle the correct word.

1. I'm looking for a pair of (jeans   necklace).

2. My favorite color is (belt   black).

3. This jacket is too (large   size).

4. What size dress do you (matter   wear)?

5. What's the (medium   price) of the shoes?

Listen and choose the correct picture. Track 33 🔊

1.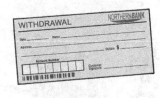
  Ⓐ Ⓑ Ⓒ

2.
  Ⓐ Ⓑ Ⓒ

3.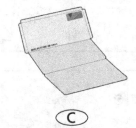
  Ⓐ Ⓑ Ⓒ

4.
  Ⓐ Ⓑ Ⓒ

5.
  Ⓐ Ⓑ Ⓒ

6.
  Ⓐ Ⓑ Ⓒ

ANSWERS			
1	Ⓐ	Ⓑ	Ⓒ
2	Ⓐ	Ⓑ	Ⓒ
3	Ⓐ	Ⓑ	Ⓒ
4	Ⓐ	Ⓑ	Ⓒ
5	Ⓐ	Ⓑ	Ⓒ
6	Ⓐ	Ⓑ	Ⓒ

1. deposit slip

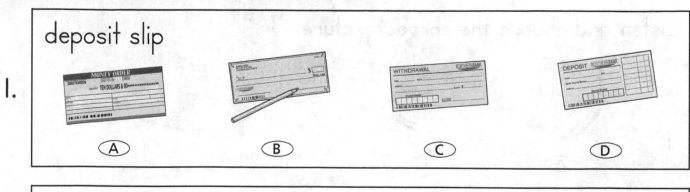

A   B   C   D

2. checkbook

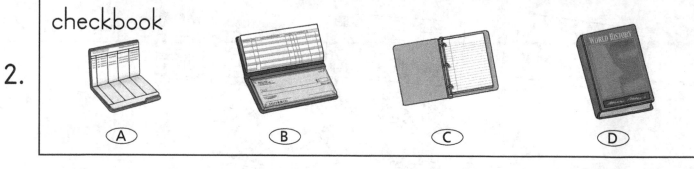

A   B   C   D

3. package

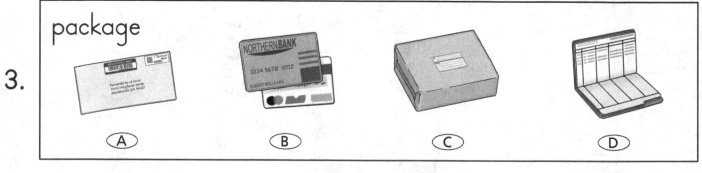

A   B   C   D

4. money order

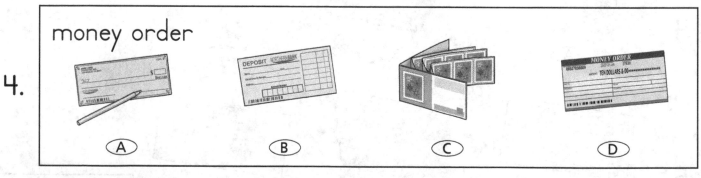

A   B   C   D

5. ATM card

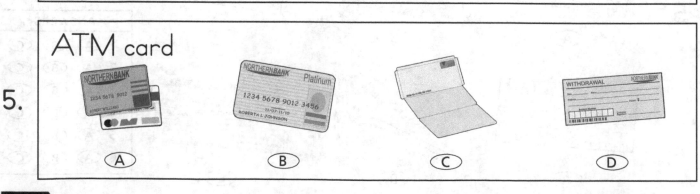

A   B   C   D

1.
- (A) package
- (B) checkbook
- (C) bank book
- (D) money order

2.
- (A) air letter
- (B) registered letter
- (C) package
- (D) deposit slip

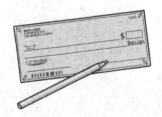

3.
- (A) money order
- (B) air letter
- (C) check
- (D) bank book

4.
- (A) check
- (B) credit card
- (C) deposit slip
- (D) withdrawal slip

5.
- (A) check
- (B) money order
- (C) air letter
- (D) withdrawal slip

6.
- (A) air letter
- (B) package
- (C) registered letter
- (D) stamp

Read, trace, and copy.

1. bank   bank

2. check   check

3. stamps   stamps

4. letter   letter

5. deposit   deposit

6. address   address

7. package   package

8. envelope   envelope

9. checkbook   checkbook

10. withdrawal   withdrawal

Make deposits and withdrawals. Your account number is 7428 1965.

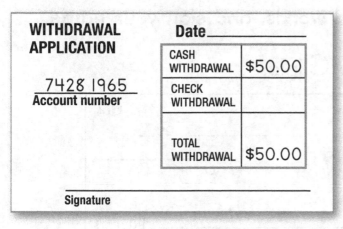

WITHDRAWAL APPLICATION	Date _____	
	CASH WITHDRAWAL	$50.00
7428 1965 Account number	CHECK WITHDRAWAL	
	TOTAL WITHDRAWAL	$50.00
Signature		

WITHDRAWAL APPLICATION	Date _____	
	CASH WITHDRAWAL	
_____ Account number	CHECK WITHDRAWAL	
	TOTAL WITHDRAWAL	
Signature		

1. Withdraw $50.00 (cash). 2. Withdraw $100.00 (cash).

WITHDRAWAL APPLICATION	Date _____	
	CASH WITHDRAWAL	
_____ Account number	CHECK WITHDRAWAL	
	TOTAL WITHDRAWAL	
Signature		

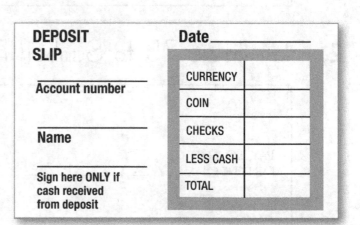

DEPOSIT SLIP	Date _____	
_____ Account number	CURRENCY	
	COIN	
Name	CHECKS	
	LESS CASH	
Sign here ONLY if cash received from deposit	TOTAL	

3. Withdraw $225.00 (cash). 4. Deposit $100.00 (cash).

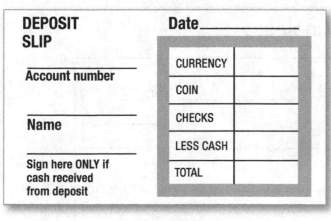

DEPOSIT SLIP	Date _____	
_____ Account number	CURRENCY	
	COIN	
Name	CHECKS	
	LESS CASH	
Sign here ONLY if cash received from deposit	TOTAL	

DEPOSIT SLIP	Date _____	
_____ Account number	CURRENCY	
	COIN	
Name	CHECKS	
	LESS CASH	
Sign here ONLY if cash received from deposit	TOTAL	

5. Deposit $20.75 (cash). 6. Deposit a check for $225.00.
Take out $25.00.

Write these checks. Write today's date, the name of the company, the dollar amounts in numbers and words, and sign your name.

1. Pay $225.00 to Midtown Clinic.

```
                                                                    142
                                      _____ 20____

PAY TO THE
ORDER OF_____  $ [        ]

_____| dollars

FOR_____     _____
0 210000021 990 507931 0142
```

2. Pay $126.75 to Sunbelt Power Company.

```
                                                                    143
                                      _____ 20____

PAY TO THE
ORDER OF_____  $ [        ]

_____| dollars

FOR_____     _____
0 210000021 990 507931 0143
```

3. Pay $67.93 to Omnitel Wireless.

```
                                                                    144
                                      _____ 20____

PAY TO THE
ORDER OF_____  $ [        ]

_____| dollars

FOR_____     _____
0 210000021 990 507931 0144
```

Circle the words. Then write the sentences.

I want to mail a package.

1. Iusemycreditcardinthestore.

2. Iwanttobuyamoneyorder.

3. Myaddressisontheenvelope.

4. Itakemoneyoutofthebank.

5. Youcanbuystampsatthiswindow.

A. Look at pages 132–133 of *Foundations*. Write the missing word.

1. deposit _____

2. return _____

3. credit _____

4. bank _____

5. money _____

6. post _____

7. registered _____

8. withdrawal _____

B. Look at page 143 of *Foundations*. Read the story and circle the correct words.

A woman is putting money in the bank. She has her bank book, a check, and a | deposit   withdrawal |[1] slip. A woman is getting money at the | checkbook   ATM |[2].

At the post office, the man on the left is buying | coins   stamps |[3]. A woman is mailing a | package   air letter |[4]. The man on the right is buying a | credit card   money order |[5].

At the supermarket, the woman on the left is writing a | deposit   check |[6]. The woman in the middle is buying food with her | credit card   envelope |[7]. The man on the right is paying with a twenty-dollar bill. His | return   change |[8] is $2.50.

A. Listen and write the number under the correct picture. Track 34

_____   _____   _____

_____   _____   _____

B. Listen and write the number under the correct picture. Track 35

_____   _____   _____

_____   _____   _____

1. cough
   A B C D

2. fever
   A B C D

3. toothache
   A B C D

4. ear drops
   A B C D

5. antacid tablets
   A B C D

1.
   - Ⓐ stomachache
   - Ⓑ backache
   - Ⓒ earache
   - Ⓓ headache

2.
   - Ⓐ fever
   - Ⓑ cold
   - Ⓒ cough
   - Ⓓ sore throat

3.
   - Ⓐ aspirin
   - Ⓑ antacid tablets
   - Ⓒ ear drops
   - Ⓓ cough syrup

4.
   - Ⓐ cold medicine
   - Ⓑ throat lozenges
   - Ⓒ cough syrup
   - Ⓓ aspirin

5.
   - Ⓐ I broke my arm.
   - Ⓑ I broke my leg.
   - Ⓒ I burned my hand.
   - Ⓓ I broke my foot.

6.
   - Ⓐ I cut my face.
   - Ⓑ I sprained my wrist.
   - Ⓒ My eye hurts.
   - Ⓓ I cut my finger.

Read, trace, and copy.

a a a a   *a a a a*

B B B B   *b b b b*

C C C C   *c c c c*

D D D D   *d d d d*

E E E E   *e e e e*

F F F F   *f f f f*

G G G G   *g g g g*

H H H H   *h h h h*

I I I I   *i i i i*

J J J J   *j j j j*

K K K K   *k k k k*

L L L L   *l l l l*

M M M M   *m m m m*

Read, trace, and copy.

Read, trace, and copy.

1. *arm*   *arm*

2. *eye*   *eye*

3. *foot*   *foot*

4. *head*   *head*

5. *neck*   *neck*

6. *fever*   *fever*

7. *cough*   *cough*

8. *finger*   *finger*

9. *stomach*   *stomach*

10. *headache*   *headache*

Write the word.

1. _____

2. _____

3. _____

4. _____

5. _____

6. _____

7. _____

8. _____

1. Take one capsule three times a day.

A   B   C   D

2. Take one tablet once a day.

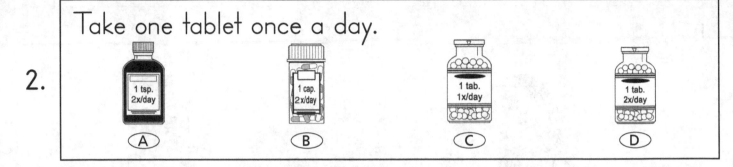

A   B   C   D

3. Take one teaspoon four times a day.

A   B   C   D

4. Take one capsule twice a day.

A   B   C   D

5. Take two pills four times a day.

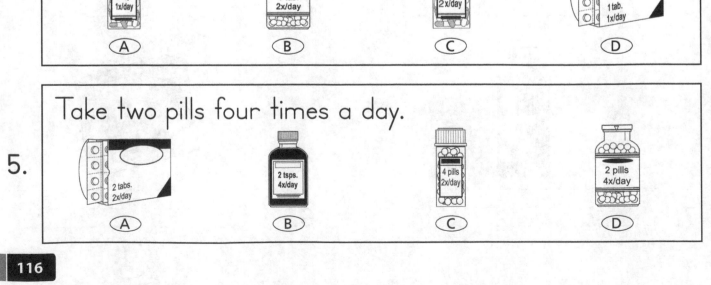

A   B   C   D

Circle the words. Then write the sentences.

I have a sore throat.

1. Shehasanearache.

2. Mystomachhurts.

3. Youshouldusecoldmedicine.

4. WherecanIfindeardrops?

5. Ithinkyoushouldtakevitamins.

A. Look at pages 144-145 of *Foundations*. Unscramble the words.

1. gle _____
2. mar _____
3. tofo _____
4. kenc _____
5. snoe _____
6. deha _____

7. dolc _____
8. reevf _____
9. hugco _____
10. gernif _____
11. hakeccab _____
12. hohotetac _____

B. Circle the correct word.

1. My (stomach   stomachache) hurts.

2. I have a sore (cough   throat).

3. When I have an earache, I use ear (drops   syrup).

4. Excuse me. Where can I find throat
   (medicine   lozenges)?

5. Hello. I want to (come in   make) an appointment.

6. I think you should take one (vitamin   meal) every day.

7. You should (eat   sleep) eight hours every night.

8. My son fell! Please send (a checkup   an ambulance)!

9. Cold medicine is in (Aisle   Doctor) Three.

10. What's the (hurt   matter)?

A. Listen and write the number under the correct picture. Track 36

___

___

___

___

___

___

B. Listen and write the number under the correct picture. Track 37

___

___

___

___

___

___

Match.

1.

2.

3.

4.

5.

6.

7.

science

music

English

social studies

math

art

technology

1. A. principal
    B. school librarian
    C. school nurse
    D. teacher

2. A. school nurse
    B. custodian
    C. guidance counselor
    D. school librarian

3. A. guidance counselor
    B. English teacher
    C. P.E. teacher
    D. school librarian

4. A. auditorium
    B. custodian
    C. principal
    D. teacher

5. A. orchestra
    B. drama
    C. choir
    D. technology

6. A. soccer
    B. gym
    C. football
    D. band

Read, trace, and copy.

1. art   art

2. math   math

3. drama   drama

4. soccer   soccer

5. library   library

6. science   science

7. football   football

8. English   English

9. orchestra   orchestra

10. cafeteria   cafeteria

Write the word.

1. _____

2. _____

3. _____

4. _____

5. _____

6. _____

7. _____

8. _____

Look at this student's school schedule. Answer the questions.

Period	Time	Class	Teacher	Room
1st	8:15–9:00	Math	Ms. Garcia	124
2nd	9:05–9:50	English	Mr. Fletcher	236
3rd	9:55–10:40	Science	Mrs. Wong	128
4th	10:45–11:30	Social Studies	Mr. Harris	312
5th	12:00–12:45	Art	Ms. Larsen	16
6th	12:50–1:35	Technology	Mrs. Ahmed	130
7th	1:40–2:25	Music	Mr. Ross	24

1. What class does this student have fifth period?
   A Math.
   B Science.
   C Art.
   D Technology.

2. Where is the Science class?
   A 4th period.
   B From 10:45 to 11:30.
   C Mrs. Wong.
   D In Room 128.

3. Which class is in Room 24?
   A Ms. Garcia's class.
   B The music class.
   C Mrs. Wong's class.
   D The art class.

4. It's 9:45. Where is this student now?
   A In Room 236.
   B In Room 128.
   C In Room 124.
   D In Room 312.

5. How long is each period at this school?
   A 30 minutes.
   B 40 minutes.
   C 45 minutes.
   D One hour.

6. What time does this student probably eat lunch?
   A From 10:45 to 11:30.
   B From 11:30 to 12:00.
   C From 12:00 to 12:45.
   D From 12:45 to 12:50.

Circle the words. Then write the sentences.

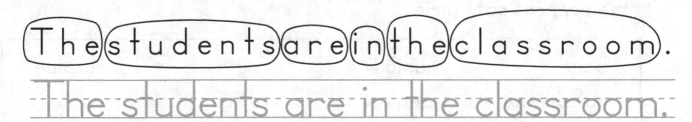

The students are in the classroom.

1. Theprincipalisintheoffice.

_____

2. Myfavoritesubjectisscience.

_____

3. Ihavefootballpracticetoday.

_____

4. Ihavemathclasssecondperiod.

_____

5. Whatareyougoingtodotoday?

_____

A. Look at pages 158–159 of *Foundations*. Write these words in the correct categories.

band	custodian	math	science
cafeteria	English	office	soccer
choir	library	principal	teacher

People at School

_____

_____

_____

School Subjects

_____

_____

_____

Places at School

_____

_____

_____

School Activities

_____

_____

_____

B. Circle the correct word.

1. My favorite subject is (auditorium   science).

2. I have (football   guidance) practice after school today.

3. My head hurts. I'm going to the (principal's   nurse's) office.

4. Basketball practice is in the (cafeteria   gym).

5. Ms. Bryant is the new (librarian   library).

A. Listen and write the number under the correct picture. Track 38 🔊

_____

_____

_____

_____

_____

_____

B. Listen and write the number under the correct picture. Track 39 🔊

_____

_____

_____

_____

_____

_____

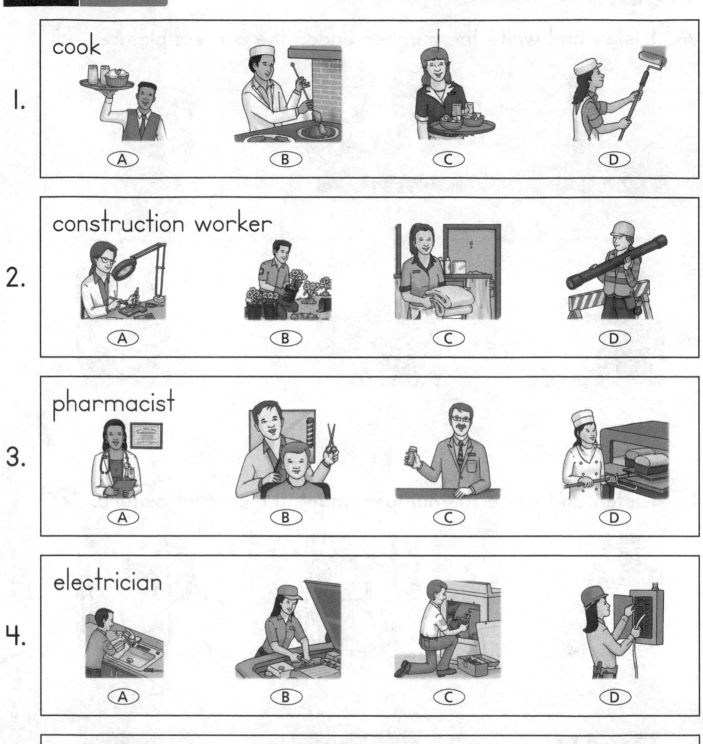

1. cook
   A   B   C   D

2. construction worker
   A   B   C   D

3. pharmacist
   A   B   C   D

4. electrician
   A   B   C   D

5. truck driver
   A   B   C   D

1.
- (A) sell clothing
- (B) operate equipment
- (C) use a cash register
- (D) cook

2.
- (A) repair things
- (B) cook
- (C) sell watches
- (D) sell clothing

3.
- (A) clean buildings
- (B) use a cash register
- (C) assemble components
- (D) sell things

4.
- (A) cut hair
- (B) operate equipment
- (C) repair things
- (D) clean

5.
- (A) employee lounge
- (B) personnel office
- (C) bathroom
- (D) supply room

6.
- (A) vending machine
- (B) mailroom
- (C) personnel office
- (D) library

Read, trace, and copy.

1. *cook* *cook*

2. *baker* *baker*

3. *doctor* *doctor*

4. *cashier* *cashier*

5. *painter* *painter*

6. *plumber* *plumber*

7. *teacher* *teacher*

8. *waitress* *waitress*

9. *mechanic* *mechanic*

10. *carpenter* *carpenter*

A. Write the word.

1. _____

2. _____

3. _____

4. _____

B. Fill out the form.

APPLICATION FOR EMPLOYMENT

Name: _____   Social Security No.: _____

Street: _____   Apartment: _____

City: _____   State: _____   Zip Code: _____   Telephone: _____

Work Experience (Start with present or most recent employer):

From	To	Job	Company
_____	_____	_____	_____
_____	_____	_____	_____
_____	_____	_____	_____

Date: _____   Signature: _____

Look at this paycheck and pay stub. Answer the questions.

Wilson's Department Store		Mercado, Y.		EMP. NO. 00427	
PAY PERIOD ENDING	**RATE**	**HOURS**		**GROSS PAY**	
10 03 14	13.00/hour	40		$520.00	

FED TAX	52.00			GROSS PAY	$520.00
FICA/MED	41.60			DEDUCTIONS	$144.10
STATE TAX	26.00				
HEALTH	24.50			NET PAY	$375.90

WILSON'S DEPARTMENT STORE　　　　　Check No.　4377291

Pay to **YOLANDA MERCADO**　　　　　Date Issued　10 08 14

THREE HUNDRED SEVENTY–FIVE DOLLARS AND NINETY CENTS————$375.90

Marjorie Denton

1. How much does this person make an hour?
   - Ⓐ $13.00
   - Ⓑ $40.00
   - Ⓒ $375.90
   - Ⓓ $520.00

2. How much does she pay for federal taxes?
   - Ⓐ $144.10
   - Ⓑ $375.90
   - Ⓒ $26.00
   - Ⓓ $52.00

3. How much are her total deductions?
   - Ⓐ $24.50
   - Ⓑ $144.10
   - Ⓒ $375.90
   - Ⓓ $520.00

4. How much does she take home after deductions?
   - Ⓐ $144.10
   - Ⓑ $375.90
   - Ⓒ $520.00
   - Ⓓ $1008.14

Circle the words. Then write the sentences.

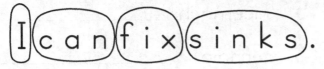

I can fix sinks.

1. Icanrepairbuildings.

2. Amechaniccanfixcars.

3. Sheworksinahotel.

4. Putonyourhelmet!

5. Thesupplyroomisdownthehall.

A. Look at pages 170–171 of *Foundations*. Unscramble the words.

1. koco _____
2. rabek _____
3. troodc _____
4. rebrab _____
5. nicemach _____
6. ternaip _____
7. drrenarg _____
8. creeyarts _____

B. Circle the correct word.

1. I'm looking for a job as a (cash register   cashier).
2. I can (drive   driver) a truck.
3. I'm an experienced (type   secretary).
4. What can you do? Tell me about your (job skills   want ads).
5. He's a (salesperson   waiter) in a restaurant.
6. Fill out the job (application   occupation).
7. I can't come to work today. I'm (the matter   sick).
8. The personnel office is across from the supply (lounge   room).
9. Put on your (safety glasses   wet floor).
10. Carlos works six (months   days) a week.
11. (Excuse me?   Careful!) Don't stand there!
12. There are many (deductions   hours) from my paycheck.

A. Listen and write the number under the correct picture. Track 40

B. Listen and choose the correct street sign. Track 41

1. ___ ✓   2. ___ ___   3. ___ ___

4. ___ ___   5. ___ ___   6. ___ ___

No right turn

1.

   Ⓐ   Ⓑ   Ⓒ   Ⓓ

Train tracks ahead

2.

   Ⓐ   Ⓑ   Ⓒ   Ⓓ

No U-turn

3.

   Ⓐ   Ⓑ   Ⓒ   Ⓓ

Don't go on this street.

4.

   Ⓐ   Ⓑ   Ⓒ   Ⓓ

School nearby

5.

   Ⓐ   Ⓑ   Ⓒ   Ⓓ

1. Ⓐ No right turn.
   Ⓑ No left turn.
   Ⓒ No U-turn.
   Ⓓ Slow down.

2. Ⓐ School ahead.
   Ⓑ Train tracks ahead.
   Ⓒ Bus station ahead.
   Ⓓ No right turn.

3. Ⓐ Don't go that way.
   Ⓑ Stop.
   Ⓒ Slow down.
   Ⓓ No left turn.

4. Ⓐ Train tracks ahead.
   Ⓑ School ahead.
   Ⓒ People in the street.
   Ⓓ Don't walk.

5. Ⓐ No left turn.
   Ⓑ No U-turn.
   Ⓒ Stop.
   Ⓓ No right turn.

6. Ⓐ Don't walk.
   Ⓑ Don't go that way.
   Ⓒ People in the street.
   Ⓓ School ahead.

Read, trace, and copy.

1. *bus*   *bus*

2. *car*   *car*

3. *map*   *map*

4. *taxi*   *taxi*

5. *walk*   *walk*

6. *drive*   *drive*

7. *train*   *train*

8. *bicycle*   *bicycle*

9. *subway*   *subway*

10. *schedule*   *schedule*

Write the word.

1. _____

2. _____

3. _____

4. _____

5. _____

6. _____

7. _____

8. _____

Look at the bus schedule. Answer the questions.

Route 6B				
Day Street	Main Street	Pine Street	Fifth Avenue	Sixth Avenue
Weekdays				
5:45 AM	6:00	6:15	6:30	6:45
6:45	7:00	7:15	7:30	7:45
7:45	8:00	8:15	8:30	8:45
8:45	9:00	9:15	9:30	9:45
10:45	11:00	11:15	11:30	11:45
12:45 PM	1:00	1:15	1:30	1:45
1:45	2:00	2:15	2:30	2:45
3:45	4:00	4:15	4:30	4:45
4:45	5:00	5:15	5:30	5:45
5:45	6:00	6:15	6:30	6:45
6:45	7:00	7:15	7:30	7:45
8:45	9:00	9:15	9:30	9:45

1. How long does it take to go from Day Street to Main Street?
   - Ⓐ 15 minutes.
   - Ⓑ 30 minutes.
   - Ⓒ 45 minutes.
   - Ⓓ 60 minutes.

2. How long does it take to go from Main Street to Fifth Avenue?
   - Ⓐ 15 minutes.
   - Ⓑ 30 minutes.
   - Ⓒ 45 minutes.
   - Ⓓ 60 minutes.

3. It's 1:00 P.M. When will the next bus leave Fifth Avenue?
   - Ⓐ 1:15 P.M.
   - Ⓑ 1:30 P.M.
   - Ⓒ 1:45 P.M.
   - Ⓓ 2:00 P.M.

4. It's 8:00 P.M. When will the next bus leave Day Street?
   - Ⓐ In 15 minutes.
   - Ⓑ In 30 minutes.
   - Ⓒ In 45 minutes.
   - Ⓓ In an hour.

Circle the words. Then write the sentences.

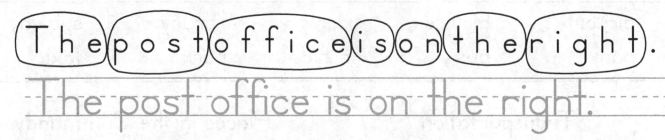

The post office is on the right.

1. Thetrainstationisontheleft.

2. HowdoIgettothelibrary?

3. TakeBusNumberOnetothepark.

4. ThehospitalisonMainStreet.

5. Lookforpeopleinthestreet.

A. Write these words in the correct categories.

airport	bicycle	car	library	subway
bank	bus	clinic	park	taxi

Transportation   Places in the Community

_____   _____

_____   _____

_____   _____

_____   _____

_____   _____

B. Look at page 189 of *Foundations*. Write the missing word.

1. No Right _____   4. _____ Way

2. Do Not _____   5. _____ Limit

3. No Turn on _____   6. _____ U-Turn

C. Circle the correct word.

1. I (ride   drive) a bicycle to work.

2. The clinic is on the (next   left).

3. The (sign   stop) says, "Do Not Enter."

4. The next bus is at 6:30. It's on the bus (number   schedule).

Listen and choose the correct picture. Track 42

 1.

Ⓐ   Ⓑ   Ⓒ

2.

Ⓐ   Ⓑ   Ⓒ

3.

Ⓐ   Ⓑ   Ⓒ

4.

Ⓐ   Ⓑ   Ⓒ

5.

Ⓐ   Ⓑ   Ⓒ

ANSWERS
1 Ⓐ Ⓑ Ⓒ
2 Ⓐ Ⓑ Ⓒ
3 Ⓐ Ⓑ Ⓒ
4 Ⓐ Ⓑ Ⓒ
5 Ⓐ Ⓑ Ⓒ
6 Ⓐ Ⓑ Ⓒ

6.

Ⓐ   Ⓑ   Ⓒ

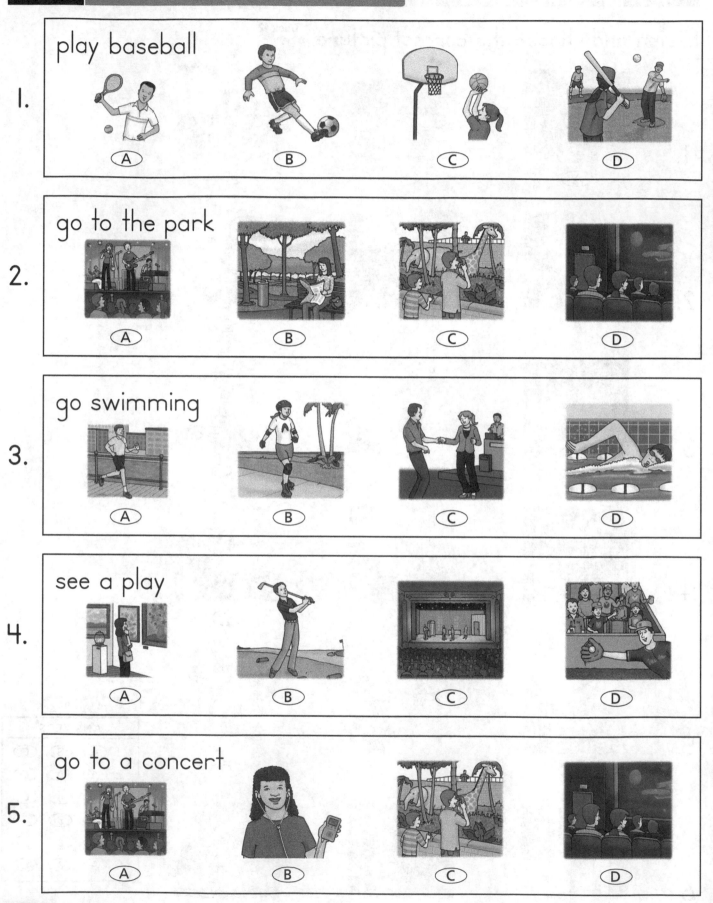

1. play baseball

   A   B   C   D

2. go to the park

   A   B   C   D

3. go swimming

   A   B   C   D

4. see a play

   A   B   C   D

5. go to a concert

   A   B   C   D

1.
   (A) play basketball
   (B) play tennis
   (C) play golf
   (D) play baseball

2.
   (A) listen to music
   (B) watch TV
   (C) go to a concert
   (D) exercise

3.
   (A) go to a museum
   (B) see a movie
   (C) see a play
   (D) go to the zoo

4.
   (A) go to a ballgame
   (B) go to the park
   (C) go dancing
   (D) go jogging

5.
   (A) play soccer
   (B) play tennis
   (C) play baseball
   (D) play golf

6.
   (A) go swimming
   (B) go dancing
   (C) go jogging
   (D) go rollerblading

Read, trace, and copy.

1. *zoo* *zoo*

2. *park* *park*

3. *play* *play*

4. *movie* *movie*

5. *music* *music*

6. *tennis* *tennis*

7. *soccer* *soccer*

8. *concert* *concert*

9. *museum* *museum*

10. *ballgame* *ballgame*

Write the word.

1. _____

2. _____

3. _____

4. _____

5. _____

6. _____

7. _____

8. _____

1. October 20, 2014

   20/14/10   14/10/20   10/14/20   10/20/14

   (A)   (B)   (C)   (D)

2. April 15, 2013

   15/4/13   4/15/13   15/13/4   4/13/15

   (A)   (B)   (C)   (D)

3. November 1, 2005

   5/1/11   5/11/01   11/1/05   11/5/01

   (A)   (B)   (C)   (D)

4. December 19, 1991

   12/91/19   19/12/91   12/19/19   12/19/91

   (A)   (B)   (C)   (D)

5. July 6, 2008

   7/6/08   6/7/08   8/7/06   8/6/07

   (A)   (B)   (C)   (D)

6. February 10, 2012

   10/12/02   2/12/10   2/10/12   10/02/12

   (A)   (B)   (C)   (D)

Circle the words. Then write the sentences.

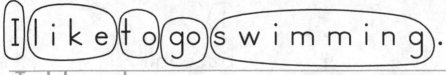

I like to go swimming.

‾‾I‾like‾to‾go‾swi‾mming.‾‾

1. Iliketoplaybasketball.

2. Sheworksfortyhoursaweek.

3. Iwenttoaconcertyesterday.

4. Iliketoexerciseinthemorning.

5. Whatareyougoingtodotomorrow?

A. Match.

1. listen to   TV
2. see a   baseball
3. watch   play
4. go to the   park
5. play   jogging
6. go   music

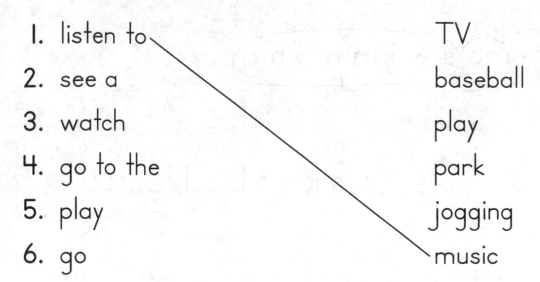

B. Write these words in the correct categories.

baseball	dancing	music	swimming
basketball	golf	play	tennis
concert	movie	soccer	TV

Sports   Entertainment

_____   _____

_____   _____

_____   _____

_____   _____

_____   _____

_____   _____

Trace.

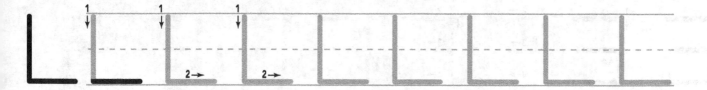

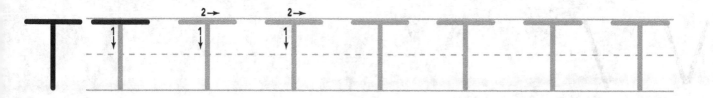

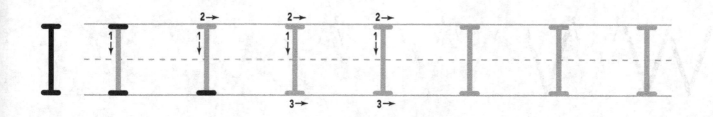

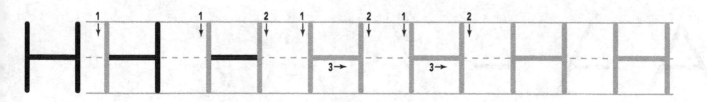

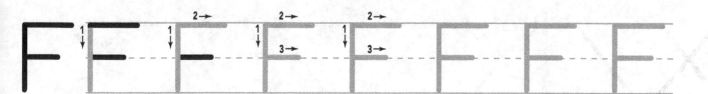

Trace.

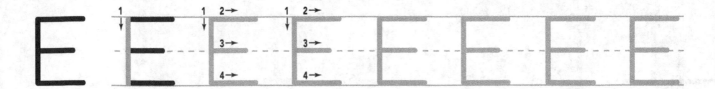

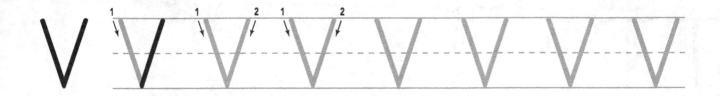

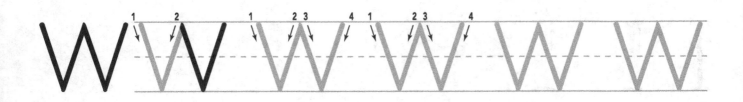

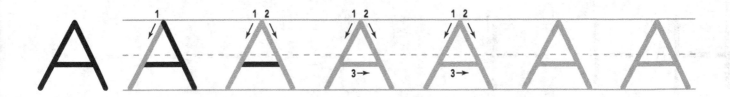

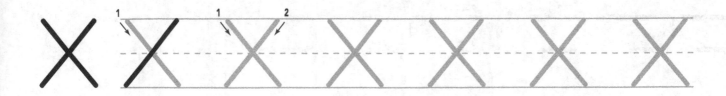

Trace.

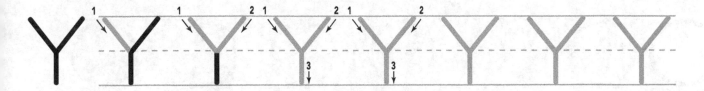

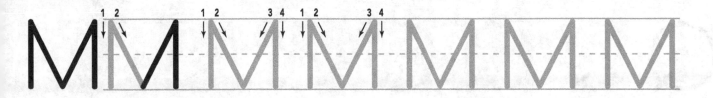

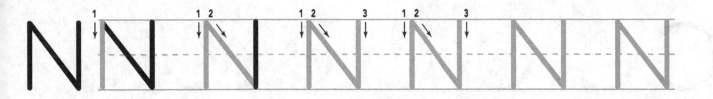

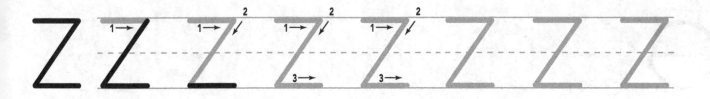

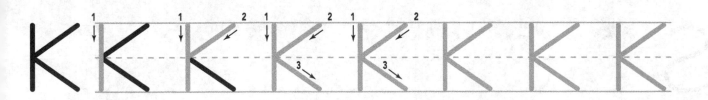

Trace.

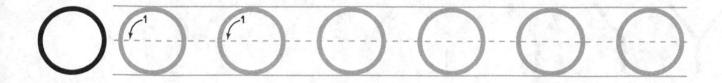

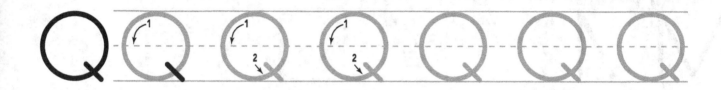

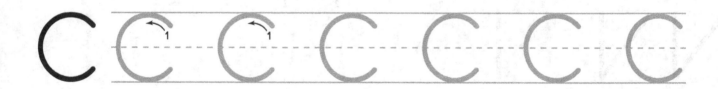

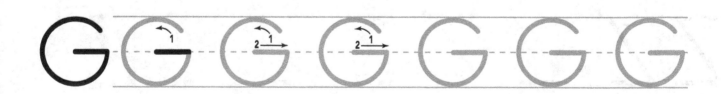

Trace.

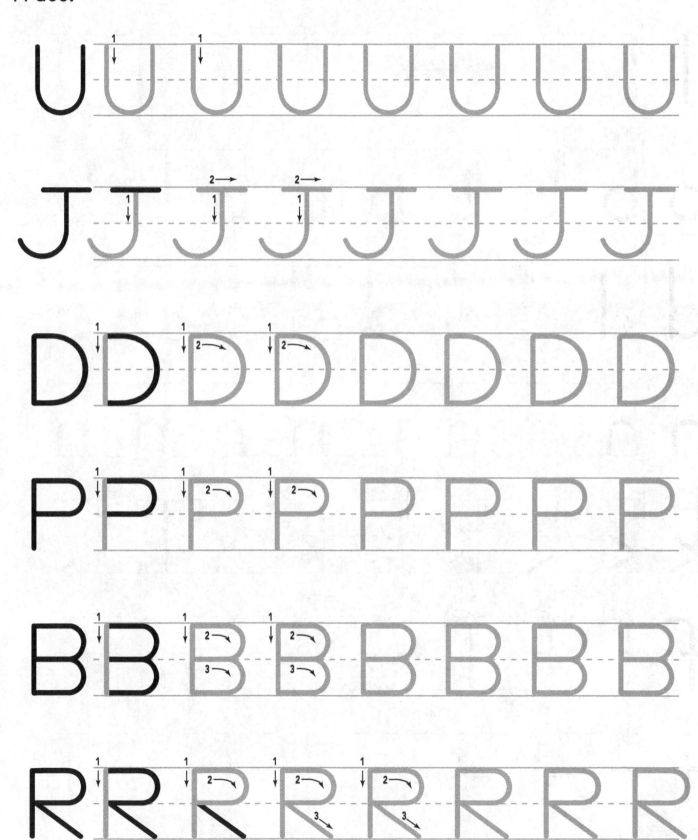

Trace.

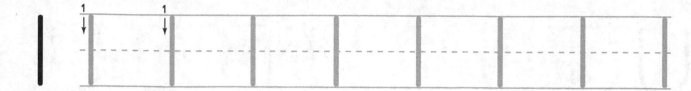

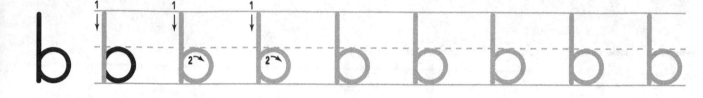

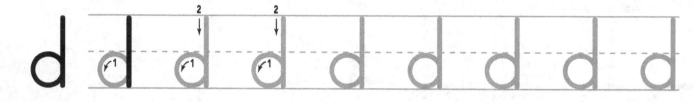

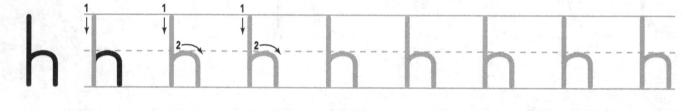

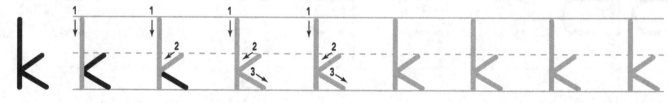

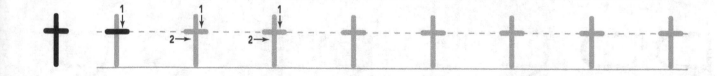

Trace.

o

c

e

a

n

m

u

Trace.

v

w

x

z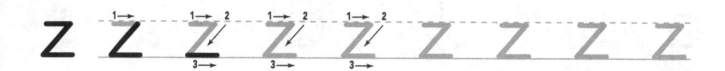

i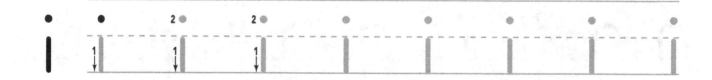

r

s

Trace.

p p p p p p p p p p

q q q q q q q q q q

g g g g g g g g g g

j j j j j j j j j j

y y y y y y y y y y

Trace.

1 1 1 1 1 1 1 1 1 1

2 2 2 2 2 2 2 2 2 2

3 3 3 3 3 3 3 3 3 3

4 4 4 4 4 4 4 4 4 4

5 5 5 5 5 5 5 5 5 5

Trace.

6 6 6 6 6 6 6 6 6 6

7 7 7 7 7 7 7 7 7 7

8 8 8 8 8 8 8 8 8 8

9 9 9 9 9 9 9 9 9 9

10 10 10 10 10 10

Page 1 Exercise B

Listen and circle the letter you hear.

1. J
2. E
3. C
4. K
5. T
6. I
7. M
8. D

Page 1 Exercise C

Listen and circle the correct name.

1. A. What's your last name?
   B. Block.
   A. How do you spell it?
   B. B-L-O-C-K.

2. A. What's your last name?
   B. Wong.
   A. How do you spell it?
   B. W-O-N-G.

3. A. What's your last name?
   B. Lewis.
   A. How do you spell it?
   B. L-E-W-I-S.

4. A. What's your last name?
   B. Asmal.
   A. How do you spell it?
   B. A-S-M-A-L.

5. A. What's your last name?
   B. Voss.
   A. How do you spell it?
   B. V-O-S-S.

6. A. What's your last name?
   B. Chen.
   A. How do you spell it?
   B. C-H-E-N.

Page 8 Exercise B

Listen and circle the number you hear.

1. four
2. seven
3. five
4. nine
5. three
6. one
7. nine
8. two

Page 8 Exercise C

Listen and circle the correct answer.

1. A. What's your telephone number?
   B. 649-2215.
   A. Is that 649-2215?
   B. Yes. That's correct.

2. A. What's your telephone number?
   B. 424-1168.
   A. Is that 424-1168?
   B. Yes. That's correct.

3. A. What's your telephone number?
   B. 825-1212.
   A. Is that 825-1212?
   B. Yes. That's correct.

4. A. What's your telephone number?
   B. 917-0025.
   A. Is that 917-0025?
   B. Yes. That's correct.

5. A. What's your telephone number?
   B. 276-1284.
   A. Is that 276-1284?
   B. Yes. That's correct.

6. A. What's your telephone number?
   B. 796-3221.
   A. Is that 796-3221?
   B. Yes. That's correct.

Page 18

Listen and choose the correct picture.

1. This is my pen.
2. This is my desk.
3. There's a clock in my classroom.
4. This is my ruler.
5. The computer is over there.
6. There's a globe in my classroom.

Page 23 Exercise A

Listen and choose the correct picture.

1. Write your name.
2. Raise your hand.
3. Close your book.
4. Sit down.

Page 23 Exercise C

Listen and circle the number you hear.

1. There are thirteen students in my English class.
2. There are twelve desks in my classroom.
3. There are sixteen chairs in my classroom.
4. There are fourteen calculators on the table.
5. There are eleven maps in my English book.
6. There are sixteen students in my English class.
7. There are seventeen books on the bookshelf.
8. There are eight computers in my classroom.

Page 29 Exercise A

Listen and write the number under the correct picture.

1. Every day I comb my hair.
2. Every day I take a shower.
3. Every day I watch TV.
4. Every day I cook dinner.
5. Every day I eat breakfast.
6. Every day I go to work.

Page 29 Exercise B

Listen and write the number under the correct picture.

1. I'm making lunch.
2. I'm washing the dishes.
3. I'm feeding the baby.
4. I'm cleaning.
5. I'm studying.
6. I'm doing the laundry.

Page 36 Exercise B

Listen and circle the number you hear.

1. I'm twenty-three years old.
2. My mother is sixty years old.
3. There are twenty-five students in our class.
4. The temperature is thirty degrees.
5. It's eighty degrees today in Los Angeles.
6. My address is 40 Pine Street.

Page 36 Exercise D

Listen and circle the number you hear.

1. My brother is fifty years old.
2. My address is 18 Lake Street.
3. There are thirty students in our class.
4. I'm thirty-four years old.
5. My father is seventy-one years old.
6. My address is 55 Main Street.

Page 43 Exercise A

Listen and circle the number you hear.

1. My address is four fifty-five River Road.
2. My address is seventeen twenty-three Main Street.
3. My address is thirty eighty-one Central Avenue.
4. My address is twelve sixteen Lake Street.
5. My English class is in Room one forty.
6. My English class is in Room three thirteen.
7. I'm in Apartment two fifty.
8. I'm in Apartment two oh four.

Page 43 Exercise B

Listen and choose the correct clock.

1. It's two o'clock.
2. It's nine thirty.
3. It's eleven fifteen.
4. It's six forty-five.

Page 48 Exercise B

Listen and circle the number you hear.

1. I live on the sixtieth floor.
2. I live on the seventh floor.
3. The English classroom is on the third floor.
4. My apartment is on the fortieth floor.
5. I live on thirty-first street.
6. This is the fifty-second floor.

Page 48 Exercise D

Listen and circle the number you hear.

1. My apartment is on the twenty-first floor.
2. My father is fifty years old.
3. I live in Apartment eighteen.
4. I live on the ninth floor.

5. Our English class is in Room ten.
6. Today is my sixth day in this English class.

Page 60

Listen and choose the correct picture.

1. The apartment has a nice bedroom.
2. This is a very nice kitchen.
3. The apartment has a nice bathtub.
4. There's a big closet in the bedroom.
5. The apartment has a very nice balcony.
6. There's a fireplace in the living room.

Page 69 Exercise A

Listen and write the number under the correct picture.

1. I'm going to the supermarket.
2. I'm going to the clinic.
3. I'm buying stamps at the post office.
4. I'm eating in a restaurant.
5. I'm going to the bank.
6. I'm going to the movie theater.

Page 69 Exercise B

Listen and write the number under the correct picture.

1. Excuse me. Where's the park?
2. Excuse me. Where's the bus station?
3. The laundromat is on Main Street.
4. The department store is on Central Avenue.
5. Excuse me. Is there a drug store nearby?
6. Excuse me. Is there a gas station nearby?

Page 77 Exercise A

Listen and choose the correct picture.

1. She's short.
2. He's young.
3. He's thin.
4. She's widowed.

Page 77 Exercise B

Listen and write the number under the correct picture.

1. He's hungry.
2. He's happy.
3. He's afraid.
4. He's sick.

Page 85 Exercise A

Listen and write the number under the correct picture.

1. I'm looking for eggs.
2. I'm looking for onions.
3. Carrots are in Aisle One.
4. Bananas are in Aisle One.
5. We need apples.
6. We need lettuce.

Page 85 Exercise B

Listen and write the number under the correct picture.

1. I'm looking for cheese.
2. Milk is in Aisle Four.
3. Sorry. There aren't any more oranges.
4. I'd like a hot dog, please.
5. I'd like a hamburger, please.
6. I'd like a taco, please.

Page 93 Exercise A

Listen and write the number under the correct picture.

1. I'm looking for a tie.
2. I'm looking for a belt.
3. Socks are over there.
4. Dresses are over there.
5. He's wearing black shoes.
6. She's wearing a white blouse.

Page 93 Exercise B

Listen and write the number under the correct picture.

1. I'm looking for a suit.
2. He's wearing a brown coat.
3. Gloves are over there.
4. What size skirt do you wear?
5. I'm looking for a blue shirt.
6. Pajamas are over there.

Page 101

Listen and choose the correct picture.

1. Where's the checkbook?
2. I need a withdrawal slip.
3. I'm looking for my bank book.
4. I want to buy stamps.
5. I want to mail a package.
6. I want to buy a money order.

Page 109 Exercise A

Listen and write the number under the correct picture.

1. I have an earache.
2. I have a stomachache.
3. I have a sore throat.
4. I have a headache.
5. I have a backache.
6. I have a toothache.

Page 109 Exercise B

Listen and write the number under the correct picture.

1. Excuse me. Where can I find ear drops?
2. Excuse me. Where can I find cold medicine?
3. Cough syrup is in Aisle Four.
4. Throat lozenges are in Aisle Six.
5. You should use aspirin for your headache.
6. You should use antacid tablets for your stomachache.

Page 119 Exercise A

Listen and write the number under the correct picture.

1. She's our English teacher.
2. He's the school librarian.
3. He's a P.E. teacher at our school.
4. She's my guidance counselor.
5. She's the school nurse.
6. He's the custodian at our school.

Page 119 Exercise B

Listen and write the number under the correct picture.

1. I'm going to the library.
2. I'm going to the auditorium.
3. I'm going to the principal's office.
4. I'm going to the nurse's office.
5. I'm going to the gym.
6. I'm going to the cafeteria.

Page 127 Exercise A

Listen and write the number under the correct picture.

1. I'm a police officer.
2. I'm a mechanic.
3. I'm a cashier.
4. I'm a plumber.
5. I'm a painter.
6. I'm a cook.

Page 127 Exercise B

Listen and write the number under the correct picture.

1. I'm looking for a job as a housekeeper.
2. I'm looking for a job as a carpenter.
3. I'm looking for a job as an assembler.
4. I'm an experienced salesperson.
5. I'm an experienced security guard.
6. I'm an experienced delivery person.

Page 135 Exercise A

Listen and write the number under the correct picture.

1. Take the C train to Pine Street.
2. Take Bus Number 2 to the train station.
3. Take the Blue Line to River Street.
4. Take Bus Number 12 to the zoo.
5. Take the B train to Park Street.
6. Take Bus Number 11 to the mall.

Page 135 Exercise B

Listen and choose the correct street sign.

1. Excuse me. How do I get to Vine Street?
2. Excuse me. How do I get to Bay Street?
3. Excuse me. Where do I get off for West Avenue?
4. Excuse me. Where do I get off for First Avenue?
5. Excuse me. How do I get to Second Street?
6. Excuse me. Where do I get off for C Street?

Page 143

Listen and choose the correct picture.

1. I like to go swimming.
2. I like to listen to music.
3. I'm going to see a play tomorrow.
4. I'm going to go to the zoo tomorrow.
5. I played tennis yesterday.
6. I went to a concert yesterday.

ANSWER KEY

UNIT 1

WORKBOOK PAGE 1

B.

1. J	5. T
2. E	6. I
3. C	7. M
4. K	8. D

C.

1. BLOCK	4. ASMAL
2. WONG	5. VOSS
3. LEWIS	6. CHEN

WORKBOOK PAGE 2

1. f	4. m
2. g	5. a
3. b	6. U

WORKBOOK PAGE 3

1. list	4. spell
2. name	5. Patel
3. your	6. Silva

WORKBOOK PAGE 8

B.

1. 4	5. 3
2. 7	6. 1
3. 5	7. 9
4. 9	8. 2

C.

1. 649-2215	4. 917-0025
2. 424-1168	5. 276-1284
3. 825-1212	6. 796-3221

WORKBOOK PAGE 9

4	four
9	nine
1	one
8	eight
10	ten
2	two
7	seven
5	five
3	three
6	six

WORKBOOK PAGE 12

1. Marta Sanchez
2. 8 Main St.
3. Los Angeles
4. California
5. 90036
6. 4G
7. (323) 723-4891
8. 223-94-9148

WORKBOOK PAGE 13

1. B	4. D
2. D	5. A
3. C	6. B

WORKBOOK PAGE 15

1. My first name is Jenny.
2. My last name is Chen.
3. My address is 6 Main Street.
4. My apartment number is 7.
5. Nice to meet you.

WORKBOOK PAGE 16

A.

1. name	5. apartment
2. first	6. number
3. last	7. social
4. address	8. zip

B.

1. father	6. wife
2. daughter	7. husband
3. mother	8. grandfather
4. grandmother	9. granddaughter
5. brother	

UNIT 2

WORKBOOK PAGE 18

1. C	4. B
2. B	5. A
3. A	6. C

WORKBOOK PAGE 19

1. globe	5. notebook
2. ruler	6. pencil
3. pen	7. map
4. computer	8. clock

WORKBOOK PAGE 20

1. C	4. A
2. D	5. D
3. B	

WORKBOOK PAGE 22

1. Sit down.
2. Open your book.
3. Write your name.
4. Raise your hand.
5. Stand up.
6. Go to the board.
7. Erase your name.
8. Put away your book.

WORKBOOK PAGE 23

A.

1. B	3. B
2. C	4. A

C.

1. 13	5. 11
2. 12	6. 16
3. 16	7. 17
4. 14	8. 8

WORKBOOK PAGE 24

1. 16	6. 18
2. 19	7. 12
3. 11	8. 13
4. 17	9. 15
5. 14	

WORKBOOK PAGE 27

1. Raise your hand.
2. Write your name.
3. The clock is on the wall.
4. Is this your notebook?
5. There are books on my desk.

WORKBOOK PAGE 28

A.

1. map	7. notebook
2. pen	8. globe
3. desk	9. table
4. clock	10. ruler
5. pencil	11. student
6. wall	12. screen

B.

1. hand	5. down
2. book	6. up
3. name	7. Take
4. board	8. Put

UNIT 3

WORKBOOK PAGE 29

A.

3	6	1
2	5	4

B.

4	3	6
1	5	2

WORKBOOK PAGE 30

1. I brush my teeth.
2. I get up.
3. I get dressed.
4. I go to school.
5. I eat lunch.
6. I exercise.
7. I play basketball.
8. I iron.

WORKBOOK PAGE 31

1. B	4. D
2. A	5. C
3. C	

WORKBOOK PAGE 32

1. D	4. A
2. B	5. C
3. D	6. B

WORKBOOK PAGE 34

1. It's raining.	5. It's cold.
2. It's sunny.	6. It's hot.
3. It's snowing.	7. It's foggy.
4. It's cloudy.	

WORKBOOK PAGE 36

B.

1. 23	4. 30
2. 60	5. 80
3. 25	6. 40

D.

1. 50
2. 18
3. 30
4. 34
5. 71
6. 55

WORKBOOK PAGE 37

1. 3
2. 60
3. 17
4. 8
5. 19
6. 50
7. 14
8. 12
9. 30
10. 53

WORKBOOK PAGE 40

1. 4
2. 8
3. 12
4. 19
5. 50
6. 80
7. 23
8. 58
9. 15

WORKBOOK PAGE 41

1. I brush my teeth.
2. I go to school.
3. Every day I make lunch.
4. What are you doing?
5. My father washes the dishes.

WORKBOOK PAGE 42

A.

1. take
2. brush
3. hair
4. breakfast
5. go
6. watch
7. bed
8. make

B.

1. wash
2. play
3. do
4. baby
5. dog
6. music
7. guitar
8. make

UNIT 4

WORKBOOK PAGE 43

A.

1. 455
2. 1723
3. 3081
4. 1216
5. 140
6. 313
7. 250
8. 204

B.

1. B
2. C
3. B
4. A

WORKBOOK PAGE 44

1. 2:00
2. 10:00
3. 3:30
4. 8:45
5. 4:15
6. 11:30
7. 7:15
8. 1:45

WORKBOOK PAGE 45

1. B
2. D
3. C
4. A
5. D

WORKBOOK PAGE 46

A.

1. Sunday
2. Tuesday
3. Thursday
4. Saturday
5. Wednesday
6. Friday
7. Monday

B.

7
6
2
5
3
4
1

WORKBOOK PAGE 47

B.

5:30   2:45   7:00   10:15

WORKBOOK PAGE 48

B.

1. 60th
2. 7th
3. 3rd
4. 40th
5. 31st
6. 52nd

D.

1. 21st
2. 50
3. 18
4. 9th
5. 10
6. 6th

WORKBOOK PAGE 49

1. 4th
2. 7th
3. 50th
4. 80th
5. 5th
6. 12th

WORKBOOK PAGE 50

1. May
2. September
3. March
4. July
5. April
6. August
7. October
8. November
9. January
10. June
11. December
12. February

WORKBOOK PAGE 51

1. A
2. D
3. D
4. C
5. A
6. C

WORKBOOK PAGE 53

A.

1. February 3, 2015
2. June 7, 2015
3. May 22, 2015
4. January 7, 2015
5. March 22, 2015
6. July 7, 2015

B.

1. April 15, 2014
2. August 20, 2015
3. October 31, 2016
4. December 21, 2017

WORKBOOK PAGE 54

A.

1. 7/12/16
2. 10/4/15
3. 6/8/15
4. 12/7/14
5. 4/10/15
6. 8/6/15

B.

1. January 14, 2015
2. June 25, 2014
3. March 7, 2016
4. September 25, 2013

C.

1. 3/12/15
2. 7/4/17
3. 5/17/16
4. 4/15/15
5. 11/16/14
6. 1/11/13
7. 9/9/15
8. 8/20/16

WORKBOOK PAGE 55

nickel	5¢
quarter	25¢
penny	1¢
half dollar	50¢
dollar bill	$1.00
dime	10¢
five-dollar bill	$5.00

WORKBOOK PAGE 56

B.

1. 20¢
2. 15¢
3. 3¢
4. 35¢
5. 6¢
6. 61¢

WORKBOOK PAGE 57

1. $25.00
2. $12.00
3. $8.00
4. $30.00
5. $70.00
6. $40.00
7. $6.50
8. $20.20
9. $11.40
10. $60.25

WORKBOOK PAGE 58

1. What time is it?
2. I am in Apartment seven.
3. My birthday is June first.
4. When do you go to school?
5. What floor do you live on?

WORKBOOK PAGE 59

A.

1. Friday
2. Sunday
3. Tuesday
4. Saturday
5. Monday
6. Thursday
7. Wednesday

B.

1. March
2. June
3. August
4. January
5. November
6. September
7. May
8. February
9. April
10. July
11. October
12. December

C.

1. March
2. July
3. May
4. January
5. October
6. December

UNIT 5

WORKBOOK PAGE 60

1. B
2. A
3. C
4. B
5. A
6. C

WORKBOOK PAGE 61

1. bed
2. chair
3. refrigerator
4. rug
5. sofa
6. lamp
7. table

WORKBOOK PAGE 62

1. B
2. D
3. C
4. A
5. C

WORKBOOK PAGE 63

1. B
2. B
3. A
4. C
5. B
6. D

WORKBOOK PAGE 65

1. kitchen
2. bathtub
3. patio
4. cabinet
5. fireplace
6. window
7. refrigerator
8. living room

WORKBOOK PAGE 66

1. 10
2. 8th
3. 2
4. 6th
5. 4
6. 3
7. 1st
8. 9
9. 2

WORKBOOK PAGE 67

1. I live in an apartment building.
2. I watch TV in the living room.
3. My apartment has a nice bathroom.
4. There is a closet in the bedroom.
5. Where do you want this rug?

WORKBOOK PAGE 68

A.

1. bed
2. rug
3. lamp
4. window
5. closet
6. table
7. sofa
8. stove
9. fireplace
10. dining room

B.

1. kitchen
2. bathroom
3. bedroom
4. patio
5. living room

C.

1. building
2. shower
3. stove
4. dining room
5. closet

UNIT 6

WORKBOOK PAGE 69

A.

5   2   4
1   6   3

B.

2   5   6
4   3   1

WORKBOOK PAGE 70

1. B
2. C
3. A
4. B
5. D

WORKBOOK PAGE 71

1. D
2. A
3. C
4. B
5. D
6. B

WORKBOOK PAGE 73

1. laundromat
2. supermarket
3. drug store
4. post office
5. gas station
6. bus station
7. shopping mall
8. grocery store

WORKBOOK PAGE 74

1. C
2. B
3. A
4. B
5. A
6. D

WORKBOOK PAGE 75

1. I am going to the post office.
2. They are eating at a restaurant.
3. The bus station is next to the park.
4. The clinic is across from the bank.
5. Is there a laundromat nearby?

WORKBOOK PAGE 76

A.

1. station
2. office
3. mall
4. store
5. station
6. theater
7. store
8. station
9. store

B.

1. post office
2. park
3. drug store
4. laundromat
5. gas station
6. restaurant
7. supermarket
8. park
9. bank

UNIT 7

WORKBOOK PAGE 77

A.

1. C
2. B
3. A
4. B

B.

4   1   3   2

WORKBOOK PAGE 78

1. happy
2. sad
3. tired
4. sick
5. afraid
6. hungry
7. angry
8. thirsty

WORKBOOK PAGE 79

1. D
2. A
3. B
4. C
5. B
6. D

WORKBOOK PAGE 81

A.

1. happy
2. sick
3. tired
4. thirsty

WORKBOOK PAGE 82

1. B
2. C
3. B
4. C
5. A
6. B

WORKBOOK PAGE 83

1. Our children are tall.
2. My brother is married.
3. She has brown eyes and black hair.
4. What does she look like?
5. What language do you speak?

WORKBOOK PAGE 84

A.

1. old
2. tall
3. heavy
4. happy
5. married

B.

1. curly
2. hair
3. height
4. sick
5. Spanish
6. Portuguese
7. China
8. from
9. language
10. middle-aged
11. hair
12. weight

UNIT 8

WORKBOOK PAGE 85

A.

3   1   5
4   6   2

B.

3   2   1
4   6   5

WORKBOOK PAGE 86

1. C
2. D
3. C
4. A
5. B

WORKBOOK PAGE 87

1. B
2. A
3. D
4. D
5. C
6. A

WORKBOOK PAGE 89

1. banana
2. cookie
3. carrot
4. tomato
5. cheese
6. butter
7. lettuce
8. ice cream

WORKBOOK PAGE 90

1. A
2. C
3. C
4. B
5. A
6. B

WORKBOOK PAGE 91

1. Oranges are in Aisle Two.
2. Are there any onions?
3. What are you looking for?
4. We need a box of cereal.
5. Please get a pound of tomatoes.

WORKBOOK PAGE 92

A.

Fruits	Vegetables
apple	lettuce
banana	onion
orange	potato

Baked Goods	Dairy
bread	butter
cookie	cheese
donut	milk

B.

1. bananas
2. loaf
3. eggs
4. bag
5. lemonade

UNIT 9

WORKBOOK PAGE 93

A.

4	6	1
2	5	3

B.

2	5	4
1	3	6

WORKBOOK PAGE 94

1. D
2. B
3. C
4. A
5. B

WORKBOOK PAGE 95

1. D
2. A
3. C
4. C
5. B
6. D

WORKBOOK PAGE 97

1. tie
2. belt
3. watch
4. skirt
5. suit
6. pants
7. jacket
8. mittens

WORKBOOK PAGE 98

1. D
2. B
3. C
4. A
5. D
6. C

WORKBOOK PAGE 99

1. May I help you?
2. The shirt is too large.
3. My favorite color is orange.
4. Watches are on the third floor.
5. What size dress do you wear?

WORKBOOK PAGE 100

A.

Clothing	Colors
dress	blue
pajamas	brown
socks	yellow

Sizes
large
medium
small

B.

1. jeans
2. black
3. large
4. wear
5. price

UNIT 10

WORKBOOK PAGE 101

1. C
2. B
3. C
4. A
5. B
6. C

WORKBOOK PAGE 102

1. D
2. B
3. C
4. D
5. A

WORKBOOK PAGE 103

1. D
2. A
3. C
4. C
5. D
6. B

WORKBOOK PAGE 105

(See page 170.)

WORKBOOK PAGE 106

(See page 171.)

WORKBOOK PAGE 107

1. I use my credit card in the store.
2. I want to buy a money order.
3. My address is on the envelope.
4. I take money out of the bank.
5. You can buy stamps at this window.

WORKBOOK PAGE 108

A.

1. slip
2. address
3. card
4. book
5. order
6. office
7. letter
8. slip

B.

1. deposit
2. ATM
3. stamps
4. package
5. money order
6. check
7. credit card
8. change

UNIT 11

WORKBOOK PAGE 109

A.

4	2	5
3	6	1

B.

5	3	6
1	4	2

WORKBOOK PAGE 110

1. B
2. D
3. C
4. D
5. A

WORKBOOK PAGE 111

1. C
2. A
3. D
4. A
5. B
6. B

WORKBOOK PAGE 115

1. earache
2. backache
3. toothache
4. aspirin
5. ear drops
6. sore throat
7. cough syrup
8. cold medicine

WORKBOOK PAGE 116

1. D
2. C
3. B
4. C
5. D

WORKBOOK PAGE 117

1. She has an earache.
2. My stomach hurts.
3. You should use cold medicine.
4. Where can I find ear drops?
5. I think you should take vitamins.

WORKBOOK PAGE 118

A.

1. leg
2. arm
3. foot
4. neck
5. nose
6. head
7. cold
8. fever
9. cough
10. finger
11. backache
12. toothache

B.

1. stomach
2. throat
3. drops
4. lozenges
5. make
6. vitamin
7. sleep
8. an ambulance
9. Aisle
10. matter

UNIT 12

WORKBOOK PAGE 119

A.

3	1	6
5	2	4

B.

6	5	3
2	1	4

WORKBOOK PAGE 120

1. English
2. art
3. science
4. math
5. technology
6. music
7. social studies

WORKBOOK PAGE 121

1. C
2. D
3. B
4. A
5. C
6. D

WORKBOOK PAGE 123

1. music / music teacher
2. custodian
3. gym / basketball
4. cafeteria
5. auditorium
6. technology
7. social studies
8. nurse's office / school nurse

WORKBOOK PAGE 124

1. C
2. D
3. B
4. A
5. C
6. B

WORKBOOK PAGE 125

1. The principal is in the office.
2. My favorite subject is science.
3. I have football practice today.
4. I have math class second period.
5. What are you going to do today?

WORKBOOK PAGE 126

A.

People at School	School Subjects
custodian	English
principal	math
teacher	science

Places at School	School Activities
cafeteria	band
library	choir
office	soccer

B.

1. science
2. football
3. nurse's
4. gym
5. librarian

UNIT 13

WORKBOOK PAGE 127

A.

3	6	5
1	4	2

B.

6	1	3
2	5	4

WORKBOOK PAGE 128

1. B
2. D
3. C
4. D
5. A

WORKBOOK PAGE 129

1. C
2. D
3. C
4. B
5. A
6. B

WORKBOOK PAGE 131

A.

1. salesperson
2. secretary
3. electrician
4. taxi driver

WORKBOOK PAGE 132

1. A
2. D
3. B
4. B

WORKBOOK PAGE 133

1. I can repair buildings.
2. A mechanic can fix cars.
3. She works in a hotel.
4. Put on your helmet!
5. The supply room is down the hall.

WORKBOOK PAGE 134

A.

1. cook
2. baker
3. doctor
4. barber
5. mechanic
6. painter
7. gardener
8. secretary

B.

1. cashier
2. drive
3. secretary
4. job skills
5. waiter
6. application
7. sick
8. room
9. safety glasses
10. days
11. Careful!
12. deductions

UNIT 14

WORKBOOK PAGE 135

A.

2	5	4
3	6	1

B.

1.		✓
2.	✓	
3.	✓	✓
4.	✓	
5.	✓	✓
6.	✓	

WORKBOOK PAGE 136

1. A
2. B
3. D
4. B
5. C

WORKBOOK PAGE 137

1. A
2. B
3. D
4. B
5. B
6. C

WORKBOOK PAGE 139

1. library
2. hospital
3. laundromat
4. bus station
5. train station
6. movie theater
7. post office
8. shopping mall

WORKBOOK PAGE 140

1. A
2. B
3. B
4. C

WORKBOOK PAGE 141

1. The train station is on the left.
2. How do I get to the library?
3. Take Bus Number One to the park.
4. The hospital is on Main Street.
5. Look for people in the street.

WORKBOOK PAGE 142

A.

Transportation	Places in the Community
bicycle	airport
bus	bank
car	clinic
subway	library
taxi	park

B.

1. Turn
2. Enter
3. Red
4. One
5. Speed
6. No

C.

1. ride
2. left
3. sign
4. schedule

UNIT 15

WORKBOOK PAGE 143

1. B
2. C
3. A
4. B
5. C
6. B

WORKBOOK PAGE 144

1. D
2. B
3. D
4. C
5. A

WORKBOOK PAGE 145

1. B
2. D
3. B
4. C
5. A
6. C

1. play golf
2. exercise
3. go dancing
4. go jogging
5. go swimming
6. play baseball
7. play basketball
8. go rollerblading

1. D
2. B
3. C
4. D
5. A
6. C

1. I like to play basketball.
2. She works forty hours a week.
3. I went to a concert yesterday.
4. I like to exercise in the morning.
5. What are you going to do tomorrow?

A.

1. music
2. play
3. TV
4. park
5. baseball
6. jogging

B.

Sports	Entertainment
baseball	concert
basketball	dancing
golf	movie
soccer	music
swimming	play
tennis	TV

1.

WITHDRAWAL APPLICATION

7428 1965
Account number

Date (Today's date)

CASH WITHDRAWAL	$50.00
CHECK WITHDRAWAL	
TOTAL WITHDRAWAL	$50.00

(Student's signature)
Signature

2.

WITHDRAWAL APPLICATION

7428 1965
Account number

Date (Today's date)

CASH WITHDRAWAL	$100.00
CHECK WITHDRAWAL	
TOTAL WITHDRAWAL	$100.00

(Student's signature)
Signature

3.

WITHDRAWAL APPLICATION

7428 1965
Account number

Date (Today's date)

CASH WITHDRAWAL	$225.00
CHECK WITHDRAWAL	
TOTAL WITHDRAWAL	$225.00

(Student's signature)
Signature

4.

DEPOSIT SLIP

7428 1965
Account number

(Student's name)
Name

(No signature)
Sign here ONLY if cash received from deposit

Date (Today's date)

CURRENCY	$100.00
COIN	
CHECKS	
LESS CASH	
TOTAL	$100.00

5.

DEPOSIT SLIP

7428 1965
Account number

(Student's name)
Name

(No signature)
Sign here ONLY if cash received from deposit

Date (Today's date)

CURRENCY	$20.00
COIN	.75
CHECKS	
LESS CASH	
TOTAL	$20.75

6.

DEPOSIT SLIP

7428 1965
Account number

(Student's name)
Name

(Student's signature)
Sign here ONLY if cash received from deposit

Date (Today's date)

CURRENCY	
COIN	
CHECKS	$225.00
LESS CASH	25.00
TOTAL	$200.00

1.

		142
	(Today's date) 20____	

PAY TO THE ORDER OF _____ Midtown Clinic _____ $ | $225.00 |

Two hundred twenty-five and ˣˣ/100 ——————————————— dollars

FOR_____ _____ _(Student's signature)_

0 210000021 990 507931 0142

2.

		143
	(Today's date) 20____	

PAY TO THE ORDER OF _____ Sunbelt Power Company _____ $ | $126.75 |

One hundred twenty-six and ⁷⁵/100 ——————————————— dollars

FOR_____ _____ _(Student's signature)_

0 210000021 990 507931 0143

3.

		144
	(Today's date) 20____	

PAY TO THE ORDER OF _____ Omnitel Wireless _____ $ | $67.93 |

Sixty-seven and ⁹³/100 ——————————————— dollars

FOR_____ _____ _(Student's signature)_

0 210000021 990 507931 0144

FOUNDATIONS

Second Edition

STUDENT BOOK / LITERACY & NUMERACY WORKBOOK CORRELATION KEY

This correlation indicates how the activity pages in this workbook coordinate generally with lessons in *Foundations* Second Edition.

	Student Book Pages	Workbook Pages		Student Book Pages	Workbook Pages
Unit 1	4–7	1–7	Unit 8	104–113	85–89
	8–11	8–15		114	90
	12–14	16		115–117	91–92
	15–17	17			
			Unit 9	120–127	93–97
Unit 2	20–25	18–21		128	98
	26–27	22–23		129–131	99–100
	28	23–26			
	29–31	27–28	Unit 10	134–139	101–104
				140	105–106
Unit 3	34–39	29–33		141–143	107–108
	40–41	34–35			
	42	36–40	Unit 11	146–153	109–115
	43–45	41–42		154	116
				155–157	117–118
Unit 4	48–51	43–45			
	52–53	46–47	Unit 12	160–165	119–123
	54–55	48–49		166	124
	56–57	50–54		167–169	125–126
	58–59	55–57			
	60–63	58–59	Unit 13	172–177	127–128
				178–183	129–131
Unit 5	66–71	60–65		184	132
	72	66		185–187	133–134
	73–75	67–68			
			Unit 14	190–197	135–139
Unit 6	78–83	69–73		198	140
	84	74		199–201	141–142
	85–87	75–76			
			Unit 15	204–209	143–147
Unit 7	90–97	77–81		210	148
	98	82		211–213	149–150
	99–101	83–84			